ONE WORLD
Teaching Tolerance and Participation

Serghei I. Cartasev

INTERNATIONAL DEBATE EDUCATION ASSOCIATION

NEW YORK * AMSTERDAM * BRUSSELS

Published by

international debate education association

400 West 59th Street / New York, NY 10019

Activity sheets may be downloaded from www.idebate.org/handouts.htm

Library of Congress Cataloging-in-Publication Data

Cartasev, Sergei.
One world : teaching tolerance and participation / by Serghei I. Cartasev.
p. cm.
ISBN-13: 978-1-932716-15-3 (alk. paper)
ISBN-10: 1-932716-15-7
1. Toleration--Study and teaching (Secondary)--Juvenile literature.
2. Prejudices--Juvenile literature. I. Title.
HM1271.K365 2006
303.3'85071--dc22
2005035704

Design by Hernan Bonomo
Printed in the USA

Contents

Introduction

The 20th century was one of dramatic change. It saw world wars, genocides, and the rise of radical ideologies based on hate. The world witnessed the appalling results of intolerance. In the last years of the 20th century, globalization changed the economic and demographic structure of the planet. National borders meant little for businesses and industries that expanded their markets and moved jobs to foreign nations. Improved communication and transportation resulted in the easy movement of people, and cities and nations became more ethnically diverse.

Our children have inherited a world in which tolerance is vital. Unfortunately, our traditional education system does not adequately prepare our children for the world they will inherit. While schools teach the academic subjects our children need to succeed, they do not teach them the practical life skills vital for living in the 21st century. In an era of globalization, children face an increasingly diverse world where radical ideologies based on hate threaten civilization. They need to understand the value of tolerance and must learn how to work together in an atmosphere of tolerance to achieve personal and societal goals.

One World offers a series of over 60 lesson plans that help students develop these skills. Students come to understand the meaning of tolerance and identify the factors that underlie tolerant behavior. For many, this will be an eye-opening experience, because teenagers often view tolerance as the appropriate behavior in dealing with people of very different backgrounds. They rarely think that they must be tolerant of their teachers, parents, or themselves! Students will also come to see that people, regardless of their background, share basic goals and concerns, and that understanding these is important for their own success and that of their community and society.

One World also teaches 21st century students how to think creatively, how to make thoughtful decisions, how to listen, and how to communicate their ideas effectively. These are skills they can apply to all aspects of their lives. In a world that is rapidly changing, they will need these skills to meet the challenges of economic globalization and to participate fully in their communities. Just as importantly, they will need these skills to create and maintain a tolerant society

Finally, *One World* teaches students the importance of participation. If they are to better themselves and their society, they must become involved in the key issues around them. They cannot be passive recipients of what their society and political order offer; instead, they have to actively work to change their world for the betterment of all. Teenagers often think that they are powerless to effect change, but in a series of lessons designed to consolidate the skills they have learned during the course, students will see that they can make a difference.

The Lesson Plans

One World is an activity-based curriculum in which students work together, using real-life situations to uncover and understand the basic principles of tolerance and to develop the life skills they need for the future. The lesson plans are based on the following principles:

1. Just as we can teach students math or science, so we can teach them the life skills they need to achieve their potential in an atmosphere of tolerance.
2. Students learn by doing. True understanding is based on experience, not memorizing facts. The activities in this curriculum allow students to experience concepts, think about their experience, and discuss it with their friends—thereby learning.
3. Learning must be practical. *One World* contains little theory. Rather, it allows students to critically analyze their own attitudes and perspectives on issues in order to develop useful, specific life skills.
4. Students must apply their skills to real situations. We cannot teach tolerance in the abstract; our lessons must be grounded in the reality the students face. They need hands-on experience, applying their skills to their personal lives. The goals they set must be based on reality, and the problems they discuss must be ones they encounter in their daily lives.
5. Activities should encourage interaction. By stimulating discussion and encouraging teamwork, the activities help students experience different opinions. Students learn that people have various viewpoints and that it is natural to disagree, but despite differences they can work together in a spirit of tolerance.
6. Activities should be fun as well as educational. Many of the activities in *One World* employ games, role playing, or drawing. Yet, though the activities are fun, each has an educational objective, often enabling students to experience concepts on a practical level. And by using these formats, students develop a sense of excitement and joy for learning. These formats create an atmosphere in which learning is both productive and fun.

The sessions in *One World* build on each other, so it is important to use them in the order in which they are presented. However, you do not need to use all the lessons. You can integrate individual parts of the curriculum in a wide range of subject areas so that students can learn these skills in courses ranging from communications to social studies and debate. Remember that this curriculum is not engraved in stone. Every classroom is different—students come with different backgrounds and have different needs. We encourage you to modify the lesson plans to meet the specific requirements of your students and ground what they learn in the reality of the environment in which they live.

Format

The curriculum is divided into three units: Tolerance, Life Skills, and Contribution. These contain the 80 lesson plans and activities. Each lesson provides the following:

- objectives
- materials needed
- opening questions (not used in final chapter)
- activities with step-by-step directions for presentation

Most lessons also include teacher tips, discussion questions, and activity or resource sheets that you can reproduce for classroom use.

PART I
Tolerance

ଔ

Chapter 1
GETTING STARTED

The first two sessions in the curriculum are designed to introduce the students to each other; create a positive, collaborative atmosphere in which all students feel comfortable contributing; and set the goals of the course.

Sessions

Getting Acquainted

Setting Priorities for Working

GETTING ACQUAINTED

This session is designed to introduce the students to each other and to create a positive atmosphere in which students will actively contribute to the class to achieve their goals.

OBJECTIVES

Upon completing this lesson, students will

1. Be able to articulate their individual goals for this class
2. Understand the importance of actively participating in the course to achieve their goals

MATERIALS NEEDED

Small pieces of various colored paper (2 pieces per student)
Flip chart or bulletin board
Tape or push pins
Poster board

TEACHER TIPS

Remind the students that they should be active, not passive, participants and that they are free to question or challenge any topic discussed in the course.

ACTIVITY

1. Introduce yourself and ask the group to form a circle.
2. Tell the students that they will be meeting each other in an unusual way. Each is to
   - say his name,
   - make a distinctive gesture,
   - name a quality of his that starts with the first letter of his name.

   After the first participant has introduced himself, the second repeats his name, gesture, and quality, and introduces herself in the same way. If the group is adventurous, the individual introducing herself can repeat the qualities of all previous participants. (This works only with small groups.)
3. After the last participant has introduced himself, ask each student to say a few words about their accomplishments, passions, qualities, aspirations, skills, hobbies, etc.

4. Explain that to get something, you must also invest something: knowledge, skills, time, wishes, energy, will, etc. Ask the students to think of the following:
   - What I want to achieve from this course
   - What I can contribute to this course

   Explain that these are their personal investments in the class. Distribute two pieces of colored paper to each participant. Tell the students to write their personal goal on one piece and their contribution on another.
5. Divide the flip chart or bulletin board into two sections: goals and contributions. Ask the students to come forward, announce their goals and contributions, and place them on the board or chart.
6. After all members of the class have announced their goals and contributions, ask the students to summarize the main themes they have heard from other students.
7. Ask the class to create a master poster of their goals and contributions that they can mount in the classroom.
8. Close the session by stressing that the members of the class create the conditions needed to achieve their goals. The class will be successful only if each individual contributes. By articulating how they will contribute, the students are on their way to making the course a success.

SETTING PRIORITIES FOR WORKING

This lesson is designed to create the collaborative atmosphere necessary for tolerance. The students determine their own goals and priorities and then use what they have learned from that exercise to establish class goals and benchmarks for achievement.

OBJECTIVES

Upon completing this lesson, students will be able to achieve the following:

1. Establish class goals
2. Identify group priorities
3. Identify reference points indicating achievement toward the goals they have set

MATERIALS NEEDED

Life Map activity sheet (copy for each student)
Our Goals activity sheet (copy for each student and each group)

TEACHER TIPS

It is important that students set realistic goals and benchmarks for themselves and the class. They should be able to see immediate benefits from their plan.

OPENING QUESTIONS

Assemble the group and ask the following questions:

1. What are your goals?
2. What makes you different from other people? What makes you similar to other people?
3. What do you need to achieve these goals?

ACTIVITY

1. Ask the students to explain how they would plan their route if they were on a vacation. Tell the students that some people have said that "life is a journey from one goal to another one." Just as they would use a roadmap to plan their route and note towns or cities to mark their progress, they can use a Life Map to set their goals and establish reference points to make sure that they are on the right course.

2. Distribute Life Map activity sheet. Ask the students to draw a simple Life Map, indicating the following:
   - Where they are (what they find important or interesting)
   - What their goals are for the next six months (they should list no more than three goals)
   - What reference points they will use to make sure they are on track for achieving their goals
   - What barriers they see standing in the way
3. Tell the students that the class can also have goals and reference points and that they will now work together to determine them. Divide the class into four groups. Ask each group to brainstorm the following:
   - **Our goals** (what we want to achieve—no more than three)
   - **Our requirements** (what we need to accomplish this)
   - **Our tasks** (what we must do to reach our goals)
   - **Our reference points** (how we know we are achieving the goals)
4. Ask each group to report back and, based on the group reports, have the class determine its goals, requirements, tasks, and reference points. Distribute Our Goals activity sheet. Tell the students to record the class decisions and keep them in their portfolios for future reference.

Activity Sheet
Life Map

Part 1

Instructions: Answer the following questions.

1. Where am I (what do I find important or interesting)?

2. What are my goals for the next six months? (List no more than three goals.)
   a.

   b.

   c.

3. What reference points will I use to make sure I'm on the track for achieving these goals?

4. What barriers do I see standing in my way, and how will I deal with them?

Part 2

Instructions:

Draw a Life Map for the next six months based on your answers above.

Activity Sheet

Our Goals

Instructions:

Record the class goals, requirements, tasks, and reference points below.

Our goals (what we want to achieve)

1.

2.

3.

Our requirements (what we need to accomplish this)

Our tasks (what we must do to reach our goals)

Our reference points (how we know we are achieving the goals)

Chapter 2
TOLERANCE AND DIVERSITY

This chapter introduces students to the concepts of tolerance and teaches them the value of diversity. The first five help the students realize how they experience tolerance and intolerance in their daily lives, understand the importance of tolerance and cooperation in achieving goals, and develop the values and skills necessary to work with others. The next three sessions help the students discover how self-understanding and appreciation of common values and other people's points of view are important in creating a tolerant society. The last four lessons teach them how to appreciate diversity, understand the harms of stereotyping, and help them communicate in an increasingly diverse world.

Sessions

TOLERANCE

What Is Tolerance?
What Is Intolerance?
Measuring Tolerance
Tolerance and Individual Rights
Creating a Climate of Tolerance

OURSELVES AND OTHERS

Self-Understanding
Ourselves and Others
Pyramid of Values

DEALING WITH DIVERSITY

The Value of Diversity
Stereotypes
Communicating in a Diverse World
Cultural Communications

WHAT IS TOLERANCE?

Individuals, families, societies, nations, and the international community cannot survive without cooperation and tolerance. This activity shows students that they cannot always act alone, and that working together makes tasks more interesting and easier to accomplish.

OBJECTIVES

Upon completing this lesson, students will be able to do the following:

1. Express their initial ideas about tolerance
2. Acknowledge the problem of intolerance in the modern world

MATERIALS NEEDED

The Meaning of Tolerance resource sheet (copy for each student)
Articles illustrating intolerance on the local, national, and international levels

OPENING QUESTIONS

1. Why do we need friends?
2. Why is it important for people to understand us?
3. Can we live without understanding each other?

ACTIVITY

Part 1: Equation for Tolerance

1. Tell the class that there is a math equation that will help them understand an important element of tolerance. Write the following on the chalkboard:

   $$1 > 2 > 4 > 8$$

   Ask the students to write down their explanation of the equation.
2. Tell each student to find a partner and discuss their explanations. Ask each pair to develop a shared explanation and suggest how it relates to tolerance.
3. Ask each pair to find another pair and have each new group of four review what the pairs have written. Tell the new groups to develop a shared explanation and suggest how it relates to tolerance.
4. Form the class into groups of eight and ask each of these larger groups to repeat the exercise.

5. Reassemble the class and ask the entire class to agree on an explanation of the equation and how they think the equation is related to tolerance.
6. Ask the class how the activity has illustrated the equation.
7. Ask the class to share examples of situations in which tolerance has helped them.
8. Ask the class to define tolerance based on their experiences.

Part 2: The Meaning of Tolerance

1. Distribute The Meaning of Tolerance and discuss.
2. Ask the students to bring in an article illustrating intolerance at either the national or the international level.
3. Have each student present the article to the class, summarizing the situation and explaining why it illustrates intolerance.
4. Once the class has completed the presentations, ask the students if they found any common themes that explain why intolerance exists. Write these on the board.
5. Ask the students if these themes are present in their school and their neighborhood.

DISCUSSION QUESTIONS

1. Can you go through life all by yourself?
2. Can you achieve your goals without collaborating with other people?
3. Can you overcome obstacles without the help of others?
4. Why is tolerance important for the family? Society?

Resource Sheet

The Meaning of Tolerance

1.1 Tolerance is respect, acceptance and appreciation of the rich diversity of our world's cultures, our forms of expression and ways of being human. It is fostered by knowledge, openness, communication, and freedom of thought, conscience and belief. Tolerance is harmony in difference. It is not only a moral duty, it is also a political and legal requirement. Tolerance, the virtue that makes peace possible, contributes to the replacement of the culture of war by a culture of peace.

1.2 Tolerance is not concession, condescension or indulgence. Tolerance is, above all, an active attitude prompted by recognition of the universal human rights and fundamental freedoms of others. In no circumstance can it be used to justify infringements of these fundamental values. Tolerance is to be exercised by individuals, groups and States.

1.3 Tolerance is the responsibility that upholds human rights, pluralism (including cultural pluralism), democracy and the rule of law. It involves the rejection of dogmatism and absolutism and affirms the standards set out in international human rights instruments.

1.4 Consistent with respect for human rights, the practice of tolerance does not mean toleration of social injustice or the abandonment or weakening of one's convictions. It means that one is free to adhere to one's own convictions and accepts that others adhere to theirs. It means accepting the fact that human beings, naturally diverse in their appearance, situation, speech, behavior and values, have the right to live in peace and to be as they are. It also means that one's views are not to be imposed on others.

Source: Declaration of Principles on Tolerance, UNESCO, 1995

WHAT IS INTOLERANCE?

This lesson teaches students that intolerance occurs on both minor and major scales. They will see how they experience intolerance in small ways in their daily lives and learn how intolerance has affected modern history.

OBJECTIVES

Upon completing this lesson, the students will be able to accomplish the following:

1. Understand that they are frequently intolerant
2. Express their initial thoughts on intolerance
3. Understand the problem of intolerance in the modern world

MATERIALS NEEDED

I'm Not Tolerant About activity sheet (copy for each student)
Impact of Intolerance resource sheet (copy for each student)

TEACHER TIPS

Activity 1: Students may want to share their personal experiences with intolerance. Be sure to be supportive. Make sure that the students understand that they do not have to share their experiences unless they want to.

Activity 2: You may want to make this a research project.

OPENING QUESTION

If all people say that they wish to be happy, and live in peace and harmony, where does intolerance come from?

ACTIVITIES

Activity 1: Intolerance in Daily Life

1. Explain that intolerance is not an abstract concept but something we deal with every day. Distribute I'm Not Tolerant About activity sheet and ask the students to complete the statements in Part 1.

2. Once the students have completed the statements, ask them to analyze their responses and see if there are any common themes. If so, list them in Part 2 of the activity sheet.
3. Have students share their responses with the class and compile a master list of factors that lead to intolerance.
4. Ask the students to develop a personal definition of intolerance based on the discussion.
5. Lead a discussion of how intolerance manifests itself in daily life.

Activity 2: Intolerance in World History

1. Explain that intolerance has had a profound impact on world history. Distribute The Impact of Intolerance resource sheet and review.
2. Tell the students to think of specific events in history that have been the result of intolerance. List these on the board.
3. Ask the students to think of the underlying causes of these events. List these on the board.
4. Ask the class if they see any common themes, and if so, ask them how they are related to intolerance.

DISCUSSION QUESTIONS

1. Are there certain things on which you and your parents will never agree? You and your friends? You and your neighbors?
2. How do you handle these disagreements?
3. Where do you think intolerance starts?
4. Are there certain forms of intolerance that are more dangerous than others?
5. Where and how should we start the fight against intolerance?

Activity Sheet

I'm Not Tolerant About

Part 1: My Intolerance

Instructions: Complete the following statements.

How I View Others

1. I don't have patience when our society______________________________

2. I don't like it when adults______________________________

3. I can't stand it when people regard me as______________________________

4. I can't stand myself when I______________________________

How Others View Me

1. I drive my parents nuts when I______________________________

2. My friends can't stand me when I______________________________

3. My neighbors don't like it when I______________________________

Part 2: Common Factors

Instructions: Review your answers to the questions above and determine whether there are any common factors that contribute to the intolerance you experience daily.

Factors:

1. ______________________________

2. ______________________________

3. ______________________________

4. ______________________________

5. ______________________________

Part 3: Defining Intolerance

My definition of intolerance is:

____

____

____

____

____

Resource Sheet

Impact of Intolerance

The 20th Century Saw

- 2 World Wars,
- 20 interstate wars,
- 20 large-scale civil wars,
- 6 major incidents of genocide,
- 100 million people killed in interstate wars,
- 100 million people killed as a result of civil wars and genocides,
- 100 million to 500 million people made refugees,
- 8 billion tons of explosives accumulated (over 1300 kg per person),
- 100,000 tons of chemical weapons developed (over 15 g per person),
- the creation of nuclear weapons capable of annihilating humankind,
- the creation of terrorist networks.

MEASURING TOLERANCE

Before students can deal with intolerance, they must be able to assess the reality of the situations they face. In working to achieve any goal, we must know the point where we start from. Tolerance starts with the ability to understand the perceptions we have and the demands we place on others and combine these with a real appreciation of our own qualities. When we are able to take the "tolerance temperature" of our society, class, family, and even ourselves, we can begin to think of ways of controlling the climate.

OBJECTIVES

Upon completing this lesson, the students will have created a tool to assess levels of tolerance and intolerance.

MATERIALS NEEDED

From Love to Hate activity sheet (copy for each student)
The Features of the Tolerant Person activity sheet (copy for each student)

TEACHER TIPS

Students may not understand why their attitudes toward themselves are important. Point out that they cannot be tolerant of others if they are not tolerant of themselves.

OPENING QUESTIONS

1. In what cases does diversity create tension in society?
2. In what cases does diversity enrich society?

ACTIVITIES

Activity 1: From Love to Hate

1. Tell the students that they can view emotions as a range from love to hate, using a scale similar to a thermometer. Distribute From Love to Hate activity sheet and ask the students to indicate on their thermometers the following:

- the average "temperature" of society
- the temperature of adults toward young people
- the temperature of the student toward others
- the temperature of the student toward him- or herself

2. Once the students have completed their individual thermometers, compile a class thermometer for each of the four temperatures. Determine the mean and average for each.
3. Ask the students to compare and discuss the results. What conclusions can they draw?

Activity 2: A Tolerant Person

1. Distribute The Features of the Tolerant Person activity sheet. Ask the class to brainstorm 10 to 12 qualities of the people in the class. Tell them to write these qualities on their activity sheets as you write them on the board.
2. Ask the students to indicate in the appropriate column which qualities they have and which qualities are needed for tolerance.
3. Compile a master list and share the results with the class.

DISCUSSION QUESTIONS

1. What did you learn about your perceptions of other people?
2. What did you learn about your perceptions of yourself?
3. In what other situations would you like to apply the tolerance thermometer?
4. How can we apply what we have learned about ourselves and our attitudes toward others to increasing tolerance in our own lives?

Activity Sheet

From Love to Hate

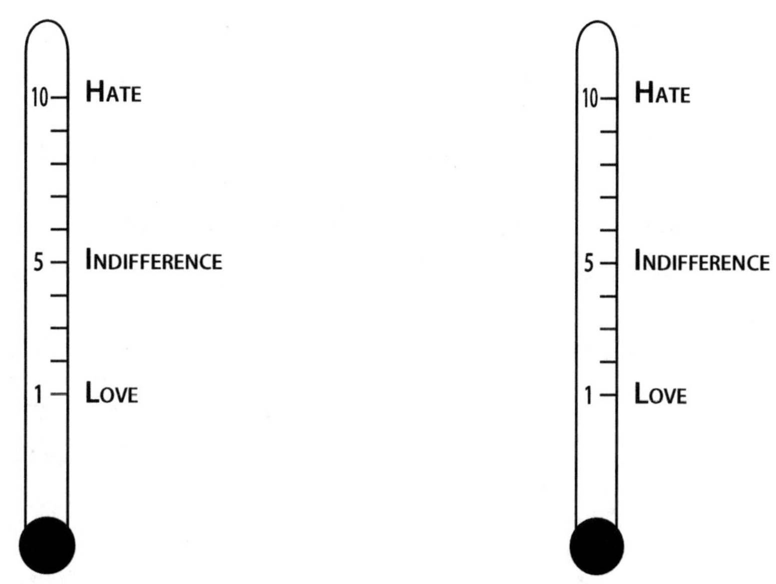

Average Temperature of Society

Temperature of Adults toward Young People

10 Hate

5 Indifference

1 Love

My Temperature toward Others

10 Hate

5 Indifference

1 Love

My Temperature toward Myself

Activity Sheet

The Features of the Tolerant Person

Instructions: Write down the 10 to 12 qualities of the people in the class as the class brainstorms them. Then check which you possess and which are important for tolerance.

Quality	I Possess	Important for Tolerance

TOLERANCE AND INDIVIDUAL RIGHTS

This lesson is designed to encourage students to investigate the status of human rights in their country and around the world. They will learn that if there is to be tolerance, they must fight for the rights of others as well as their own.

OBJECTIVES

Upon completing this lesson, students will understand that tolerance can only be achieved when individual rights are respected.

MATERIALS NEEDED

Our Rights activity sheet (copy for each student)

OPENING QUESTIONS

1. Why do we need rights?
2. What are the differences between (a) the legal protection of a right; (b) a general respect for a right; and (c) the full realization of a right?

ACTIVITY

1. Distribute Our Rights activity sheet. Ask the class to think of 10 important rights and enter them on the activity sheet.
2. Tell the students to evaluate the status of each right for their country and for nations in general. Is it protected by law? Does the general population respect it? Do all people have this right or must we continue to fight for it?
3. Once the class has completed the activity sheet, compile a master list of rights and ask the students to discuss the status of each.
4. Write the following on the board and discuss with the class.

   Tolerance: everyone wins when I realize my rights

   Intolerance: everyone looses when I must fight for my rights

DISCUSSION QUESTIONS

1. What conclusions can we draw from this exercise?
2. Do you know enough about the status of other people's rights?

Activity Sheet

Our Rights

Instructions:

1. List 10 important rights in the first column.
2. Evaluate the status of each right for our country and for nations in general.
    - Is it protected by law?
    - Does the general population respect it?
    - Do all people have this right or must we continue to fight for it?

Right	Protected by Law (inadequately, adequately, fully)		Respected by Population (inadequately, adequately, fully)		All People Have this Right (yes, no)	
	My Country	Other Countries	My Country	Other Countries	My Country	Other Countries
1.						
2.						
3.						
4.						
5.						
6.						
7.						
8.						
9.						
10.						

CREATING A CLIMATE OF TOLERANCE

Students cannot develop tolerance unless they have the necessary skills to deal with different people and difficult situations. This lesson helps them build the values and skills needed to work harmoniously with others.

OBJECTIVES

Upon completing this lesson, students will be able to do the following:

1. Create models of tolerant behavior
2. Define the principles of tolerance

MATERIALS NEEDED

Values for Tolerance resource sheet

TEACHER TIPS

You can use Values for Tolerance resource sheet to help students develop their values list, or you could distribute the sheet and use it as the basis for a class discussion.

OPENING QUESTIONS

Did you ever amicably settle a difficult problem with someone? How did you feel?

ACTIVITIES

Activity 1: Role Playing

1. Organize the class into small groups and assign each group a role: company, family, youth group, community organization.
2. Ask each group to develop a situation they would like to role play (family event, business situation, common project, etc.), and assign roles to each member of the group.
3. Assign each group a problem or conflict situation.
4. Tell the students to deal with the problem based on the roles they have been assigned.
5. Once the groups have finished their role plays, have them report back to the class. Did some of the participants' actions make dealing with the problem difficult? Easy? Did some behavior contribute to tolerance?

Activity 2: Friends and Enemies

1. Divide the class into four groups and ask each to brainstorm the following questions:

    Group 1: What do you need to turn an enemy into a friend?

    Group 2: What do you have to do to prevent a friend from becoming an enemy?

    Group 3: What values are needed for tolerance?

    Group 4: What values are needed for collaboration?

2. Ask the groups to present their findings to the entire class.
3. Write the following on the board and discuss with the class.

    Tolerance: everyone wins

    Intolerance: everyone wants someone else to lose

4. Ask the class to develop Values for Tolerance based on the groups' findings.

DISCUSSION QUESTIONS

1. What insights have you gained from this activity?
2. How can you transfer what you have learned here to real-life situations?

Resource Sheet

Values for Tolerance

A tolerant person has the following characteristics:

- Accepts the individuality of a person or community
- Respects others' opinions and points of view
- Acknowledges the positive qualities of others
- Controls one's own emotions
- Respects others' privacy and "non-interference" zone
- Looks for common interests and goals
- Respects ethical norms
- Acts responsibly toward others
- Maintains a balance between competition and cooperation
- Avoids preconceived notions and the use of negative stereotypes
- Is open to new ways of thinking
- Admits ones own mistakes
- Works to complement the individual qualities of the partners
- Balances individual desires with societal needs
- Avoids characterizing people in absolute
- Adjusts his actions to meet particular situations
- Looks for positive results
- Works with all the parties involved in a situation
- Tries to find compromises
- Respects the value of diversity
- Respects the rights of others
- Fights all kinds of intolerance
- Renounces force and violence
- Looks at the harmony of existence

SELF-UNDERSTANDING

Self-understanding is vital to the development of a tolerant society. Unless we understand ourselves, we cannot understand how we fit into our communities, nations, and the world in general. We cannot identify with others and realize what all humans have in common. Self-understanding also helps us overcome obstacles, deal with crises, and achieve our goals. In this lesson, students begin the process of self-identification by using the analogy of a nation state.

OBJECTIVES

Upon completing this lesson, students will understand the following:

1. They are unique individuals
2. There are issues important to them

MATERIALS NEEDED

My Country activity sheet (copy for each student)

TEACHER TIPS

Emphasize that students must respect each other's opinions. They have the right to disagree, but they do not have the right to be disagreeable.

OPENING QUESTIONS

1. How does a country determine its foreign policy?
2. How do people determine what issues are important to them?

ACTIVITY

1. Explain to the students that in this activity they are to view themselves as nations. Like countries, they have a name, a history, and other attributes that make them unique and symbolize how they want others to see them.
2. Distribute My Country activity sheet and ask the students to complete Part 1.

3. Tell the students that just as nations have foreign policies that determine how they act toward other states, their "country" has policies that determine how they act toward others. Ask the students to write the basic elements of their "foreign policy" in Part 2 of the activity sheet.
4. Tell the students that nations frequently have issues about which they feel strongly and which they will defend. Ask them to list their important issues in Part 3 of the activity sheet.
5. Ask students to share the characteristics of their "countries" with the class. What are their nations' vital issues?

DISCUSSION QUESTIONS

1. How did you feel when you stood up for your opinion?
2. How did you feel when you didn't stand up for your position?
3. How do you think people see you when you stand up for your beliefs?

Activity Sheet

My Country

Part 1:

Instructions: Complete the following description of your "country."

Name: ______________________________

What My Name Means to Me:

____

____

____

My Plant (the plant you would be):

My Animal (the animal you would be):

My National Symbol:

My Motto:

My National Anthem:

History (important events in your life):

____

____

____

____

____

____

Part 2:

Instructions: Explain the basic tenets of your "country's" "foreign policy" toward others.

Basic Tenets of My Foreign Policy

____

____

____

____

____

Part 3:

Instructions:

1. List your "country's" areas of vital interest and the opinions it will defend.
2. Write a paragraph describing an incident in which you have defended an opinion.

Opinions I Will Defend

____

____

____

____

____

When I Defended My Opinion

____

____

____

____

____

____

OURSELVES AND OTHERS

To create a tolerant society, we must understand how people's points of view impact each other and society as a whole. This exercise uses the analogy of a mosaic to encourage students to explore this topic. They will appreciate the importance of maintaining their own positions while working for a better society and of accepting and working with people with whom they may disagree.

OBJECTIVES

Upon completing this lesson, students will understand the following:

1. How the views they have impact their society
2. How other people's views impact them

MATERIALS NEEDED

Activity 1:
Small pieces of colored paper in different shapes
Tape
Flip chart or large piece of construction paper

Activity 2:
Ourselves and Others activity sheet (copy for each student)

OPENING QUESTIONS

1. What is a mosaic?
2. How is society like a mosaic?

ACTIVITIES

Activity 1: Mosaic

1. Explain that in this lesson you will use the analogy of a mosaic to illustrate how people's views impact society and vice-versa.
2. Give each student a few small pieces of colored paper.
3. Ask the students to come up one by one and tape their papers on the flip chart in a way they think would make the best mosaic for the entire class. Do not allow the students to discuss where they will place their pieces.

4. Tell the students that each piece of paper represents an individual viewpoint and that the mosaic represents society.
5. Ask the students the following questions:
   - Would we have had a similar mosaic if the papers were arranged differently? Using our analogy, relate this question to individual viewpoints and society.
   - Could we have developed an integrated, attractive, and interesting mosaic if each student had not worked to make it the best mosaic possible? Again, using our analogy, what does this say about how people should work in society?
   - What would have happened if each of us had tried to make his or her own best mosaic rather than the best mosaic for the class? Relate this to viewpoints in society.
   - What does the mosaic say about tolerance in society?

Activity 2: Trust

1. Explain that frequently our attitudes about ourselves and others prevent us from working together.
2. Distribute Ourselves and Others activity sheet. Tell the students to write a particular area of their lives (family, politics) in the appropriate spaces below.
3. Ask the students to indicate on each scale the percent of time they trust their own positions and those of others, and how often they think other people trust theirs.
4. Ask the students to analyze their findings. What do their findings say about their tolerance?

DISCUSSION QUESTIONS

1. How does society influence your opinions?
2. How can you influence the positions society takes?
3. Do you have to give up your own positions for the good of society?
4. How should you work with people who hold different opinions?

ACTIVITY SHEET

OURSELVES AND OTHERS

Instructions:

1. Write a particular area of your life (family, politics) in the appropriate spaces below.

2. Indicate on each scale the percent of time you trust your own positions and those of others, and how often you think other people trust yours. Write the number in the appropriate box.

AREA: ____

I trust my own viewpoints _____% of the time.

1% 10% 20% 30% 40% 50% 60% 70% 80% 90% 100%

I trust other people's viewpoints _____% of the time.

1% 10% 20% 30% 40% 50% 60% 70% 80% 90% 100%

Other people trust my viewpoints _____% of the time.

1% 10% 20% 30% 40% 50% 60% 70% 80% 90% 100%

AREA: ____

I trust my own viewpoints _____% of the time.

1% 10% 20% 30% 40% 50% 60% 70% 80% 90% 100%

I trust other people's viewpoints _____% of the time.

1% 10% 20% 30% 40% 50% 60% 70% 80% 90% 100%

Other people trust my viewpoints _____% of the time.

1% 10% 20% 30% 40% 50% 60% 70% 80% 90% 100%

AREA: ____

I trust my own viewpoints _____% of the time.

1%	10%	20%	30%	40%	50%	60%	70%	80%	90%	100%
I	I	I	I	I	I	I	I	I	I	I

I trust other people's viewpoints _____% of the time.

1%	10%	20%	30%	40%	50%	60%	70%	80%	90%	100%
I	I	I	I	I	I	I	I	I	I	I

Other people trust my viewpoints _____% of the time.

1%	10%	20%	30%	40%	50%	60%	70%	80%	90%	100%
I	I	I	I	I	I	I	I	I	I	I

PYRAMID OF VALUES

Developing tolerance requires students to understand their own values as well as those that they share with their community and all people. In this lesson the students complete two exercises that help them determine their values. They then rank these values in a pyramid and compare them to values they believe their community or nation thinks important and to those they think all people hold.

OBJECTIVES

Upon completing this lesson, the students will be able to articulate their values and rank them in a pyramid.

MATERIALS NEEDED

Pyramid of Values activity sheet (copy for each student)

TEACHER TIPS

This session is fundamental to this course but may be difficult for students because they have never analyzed their values. Completing this exercise first as a class will help them understand what they must do when they complete it individually. Students may need help in thinking through their pyramids but may be reluctant to share the personal thoughts on which their pyramid is based. Do not insist that they answer all questions fully. The goal of this exercise is to help students begin thinking about what values are important to them.

OPENING QUESTIONS

1. What is a value?
2. Why are values important?
3. How do we develop our values?

ACTIVITY

1. Distribute Pyramid of Values activity sheet and ask the students to complete Part 1. Tell the students to think of five things they want from life and write them in the left-hand column. Then ask them to complete the right-hand column describing what they would give up to have what they wanted.

2. Ask the class to complete the questionnaire in Part 2 of the activity sheet.
3. Have the students share their answers to Parts 1 and 2. Lead a discussion on what their answers reveal about their values. Remember not to press students who may be reluctant to participate.
4. Tell the students to use their answers to Parts 1 and 2 of the activity sheet to determine the values they find important and then list them in the first column of the Key Values chart.
5. Ask the students to write the values they think their community or nation believes important in the second column. Then tell them to list the values all people think important in the last column.
6. Lead a discussion of the Key Values chart. Is there any overlap among columns? Why?
7. Ask the students to rank their Key Values on a pyramid and justify their ranking.

DISCUSSION QUESTIONS

1. What values do we have in common?
2. What roles do values play in our lives and the lives of our community and world?

Activity Sheet

Pyramid of Values

Part 1:

Instructions: Think of five things you want from life and write them in the left-hand column. Then describe what you would give up to have what you wanted in the right-hand column.

What I Want from Life	What I Would Give Up
1.	
2.	
3.	
4.	
5.	

Part 2:

Instructions: Complete the following questionnaire.

1. What gives you the greatest pleasure in your life?
    a.
    b.
    c.

2. What do you like most about yourself?
    a.
    b.
    c.

3. What things can't you do without?
    a.
    b.
    c.

4. What things must everyone have?
    a.
    b.
    c.

5. What is most important in human relationships?
    a.
    b.
    c.

6. For what are you ready to pay any amount of money?
    a.
    b.
    c.

7. For what are most people ready to pay money?
   a.
   b.
   c.

8. What are some things that money can't buy?
   a.
   b.
   c.

9. What do we need to keep people acting human?
   a.
   b.
   c.

10. For what are you ready to fight to the death?
   a.
   b.
   c.

11. For what would you give up everything?
   a.
   b.
   c.

12. For what do you think people around the world would give up everything?
   a.
   b.
   c.

Part 3:

Instructions: Based on your answers in Parts 1 and 2, list the personal values you think important. Then list the values you believe people in your community or nation and all people think essential.

KEY VALUES

My Personal Values	My Community's Values	Human Values

Part 4:
Instructions: Rank your important values on the pyramid below and explain your ranking.

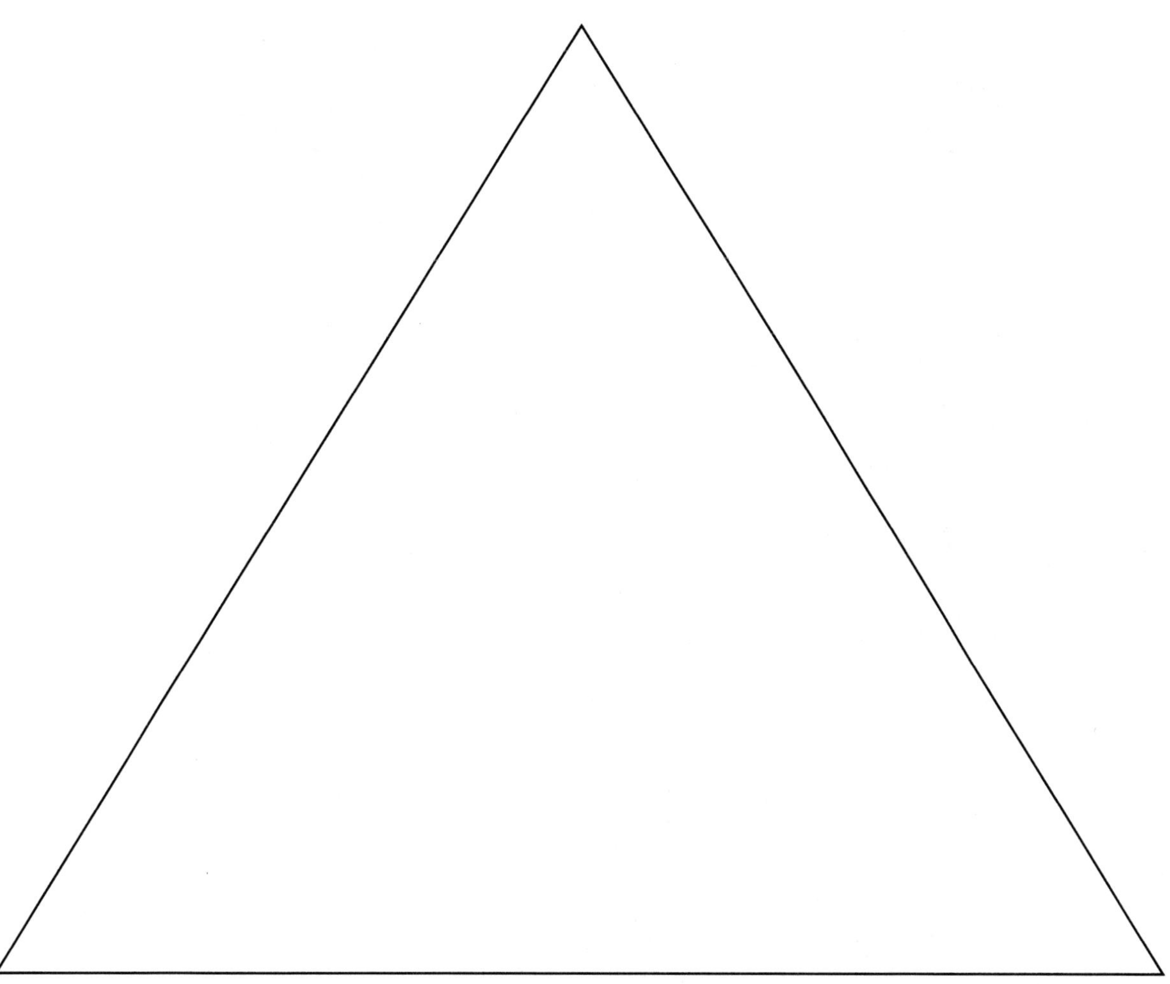

Why I Ranked My Values as I Did

THE VALUE OF DIVERSITY

This lesson teaches students that the most valuable asset of any society is the diversity of its population. If everyone were identical, with identical qualities and abilities, life would lose its beauty and development would stop. If people had nothing in common, society would devolve into chaos. Every person contributes to the development of society, but only when people embrace tolerance can society live peacefully and develop efficiently.

OBJECTIVES

Upon completing this lesson, students will understand that diversity is one of a society's main assets.

MATERIALS NEEDED

Pieces of colored paper cut or torn into unique shapes and sizes
Large piece of poster board

TEACHER TIPS

If the class is large, you may need to divide the students into groups.

OPENING QUESTIONS

1. What does uniformity mean?
2. What does diversity mean?
3. Are their things you like about uniformity? Dislike?
4. Are their things you like about diversity? Dislike?
5. Can uniformity and diversity become harmful? How and when?

ACTIVITY

1. Give each student a piece of colored paper. Ask the class to create a beautiful picture using all the pieces of paper.
2. Once the class has completed the project, ask the students how they developed the picture. Ask them how their collaborative effort illustrates important elements of tolerance.

3. Ask the class how the picture illustrates the importance of diversity.
   - Could they have created the same picture if all the pieces had been identical?
   - Could they have created the same picture if the pieces had been scattered at random with no effort to interrelate them?
4. Ask the students to write an essay explaining how their picture is a pictorial representation of individuals in society.

DISCUSSION QUESTIONS

1. What would life be like if all people were absolutely identical?
2. What would life be like if all people had nothing in common?
3. What is the value of diversity?

FOLLOW-UP EXERCISE

Debate the topic: A society's most valuable asset is its diversity.

STEREOTYPES

One extremely important element in developing tolerance is understanding the often negative role that stereotyping plays in contemporary society. Students need to know not only that stereotyping alienates people and leads to social tension, but that it also prevents them and society in general from achieving their goals. In this lesson, teenagers address prejudice directly. It is a very sensitive topic that you must handle carefully. Nevertheless, we cannot avoid it if we are to build a tolerant society.

OBJECTIVES

Upon completing this lesson, students will achieve the following:

1. Understand the problems associated with stereotyping
2. Begin developing the skills to counter stereotyping

MATERIALS NEEDED

Stereotypes resource sheet (copy for each student)

TEACHER TIPS

This can become a very sensitive lesson. If students become emotional or do not treat the exercise with respect, intervene immediately.

OPENING QUESTIONS

1. What are preconceptions?
2. What is a stereotype?
3. Why do people stereotype others?

ACTIVITY

Part 1: Picture of Prejudice

1. Ask the students to draw a picture of prejudice. It can be abstract or representational.
2. Exhibit the pictures and lead a discussion based on what the students have drawn.

Part 2: Stereotypes

1. Divide the class into pairs and assign each pair a category and role from the Stereotypes resource sheet, or use any other categories you think important.
2. Ask each pair to sit face to face and assume their roles.
3. Have one person from each pair tell his partner about the stereotypes and preconceptions associated with his assigned role.
4. Have that same student listen to his partner's opinion of people in his category.
5. Have the other student in the pair repeat steps 3 and 4.
6. Reassemble the class and lead a discussion based on the exercise.

Part 3: Preconceptions

1. Divide the class into four teams and assign each a category: religion, ethnicity, age, and sex. Have each team list the preconceptions and stereotypes associated with their category. Then ask them to suggest ways to counter the various stereotypes.
2. Have each team report back to the class.

DISCUSSION QUESTIONS

1. What are the problems with using stereotypes?
2. Are there any benefits in stereotyping?
3. Why is it difficult for people to rid themselves of stereotypes?
4. What can we do to prevent ourselves from stereotyping others?
5. What can we do to protect ourselves from stereotyping?

Stereotypes

Possible Pairings for Activity

People of two nationalities (American and Saudi)

People of two age groups (14–18 and 75–85 years)

Man and woman

People of different religions (your choice)

People of different socioeconomic groups

People of two races (your choice)

Fans of country music and of classical music

Thin and fat people

City dwellers and suburban dwellers

People from a Southern state and from a Northern state

People from different political parties

COMMUNICATING IN A DIVERSE WORLD

As our society grows more diverse, the problems of communicating with various groups become more difficult. To create a tolerant society, students need to know which factors facilitate communication and which impede it. They must also learn to search for common ground that can defuse situations of intolerance and conflict. In this lesson they analyze these factors and discover the importance of understanding and respecting people's values and viewpoints when communicating. Finally, they will learn to search for those values that people have in common or that can lead to compromise.

OBJECTIVES

Upon completing this lesson, the students will be able to accomplish the following:

1. Articulate the values that facilitate or impede communication
2. Understand the importance of people's values in communication
3. Understand the importance of focusing on those values that all people have in common
4. Understand the importance of finding those values that can lead to compromise

MATERIALS NEEDED

Communicating in a Diverse World activity sheet (copy for each student)

OPENING QUESTIONS

Why is it so difficult to communicate with people who are different from you—like your parents?

ACTIVITY

1. Divide the class into four teams and assign each a category: religion, ethnicity, age, and sex.
2. Divide each team into two subgroups: "We" and "They." Assign each subgroup additional characteristics. For example, all "We's" might be poor and all "They's" wealthy.
3. Ask each subgroup to determine its basic values. Have the members discuss these values with the members of the other subgroup in their team.

4. Ask each subgroup to describe the other subgroup as if the other subgroup were its enemy. Its friend.
5. Ask each team to analyze the similarities between its "We's" and "They's."
6. Ask each team to determine how its "We's" and "They's" can complement each other. What can each subgroup contribute to the other?
7. Ask each team to determine the values that might make it difficult for the "We's" and "They's" to communicate. What can each subgroup do to overcome these difficulties?
8. Ask each team to answer this question: If you had to recommend one thing that would ensure better communication between your subgroups, what would that be?
9. Assemble the class and ask each team to report its findings. Lead a discussion based on the findings.

DISCUSSION QUESTIONS

1. What values do all groups have in common?
2. About what do most groups disagree?
3. What is the major stumbling block to communication?

Activity Sheet

Communicating in a Diverse World

My team's subgroups: ___________________ & ___________________

My subgroup: _____________________

My Subgroup's Basic Values	The Other Subgroup's Basic Values
1.	1.
2.	2.
3.	3.
4.	4.
5.	5.
6.	6.
7.	7.
8.	8.
9.	9.
10.	10.

Description of the Other Group as Enemy:

Description of the Other Group as Friend:

Values We Share	Values That Complement My Group	Values That Might Make Communication Difficult
1.		
2.		
3.		
4.		
5.		

The One Thing That Will Ensure Better Communication with the Other Group Is:

CULTURAL COMMUNICATIONS

Tolerance is based on understanding. In this lesson students will research various nations and ethnic groups so that they can better understand diverse cultures and customs and their contributions to the world, and begin to appreciate cultural differences.

OBJECTIVES

Upon completing this lesson, the students will have learned about the cultures and customs of various ethnic groups and their contributions to society.

MATERIALS NEEDED

Cultural Communications activity sheet (copy for each student)

TEACHER TIPS

Make sure that the students study the cultures and nationalities represented in the class, but do not have students research their own ethnic group.

OPENING QUESTIONS

1. Why is there so much ethnic conflict in the world?
2. Why do you think various ethnic groups often misunderstand each other?

ACTIVITY

1. Distribute Cultural Communications activity sheet and review.
2. Assign each student an ethnic group or nationality to research. Alternatively, students can choose the group they want to investigate. Make sure they do not research their own ethnic group.
3. Give the students a week to research their projects and then report their findings.
4. Ask all the members of the class to illustrate how their culture would: greet someone; say "yes" or agree with someone; and say "no" or disagree with someone.

5. Ask a student who has investigated a northern European culture and a student who has studied a Mediterranean or Middle Eastern culture to come to the front of the room and have a conversation about a controversial topic (it could be anything), acting the way a person from the culture they studied would act. How do the cultures differ in terms of personal space, animation, etc.?

DISCUSSION QUESTIONS

1. Why is it important that people understand different cultures?
2. What do we mean when we say, "Different nationalities, languages, cultures, and traditions are humanity's common treasure"? Do you agree or disagree with this statement?
3. How has globalization affected our understanding of different cultures?

Activity Sheet

Cultural Communications

Nationality or Ethnic Group: ______________________________

Instructions: Describe the following.
Language:

Religion:

Foods:

Greetings and Introductions:

Use of Gestures:

Holidays and Traditions:

Cultural Do's and Don'ts:

Contribution to History:

PART II
Life Skills

CHAPTER 3
INTERESTS, SKILLS, AND GOALS

The lessons in Chapter 3 help students begin the process of self-examination needed to understand their interests and articulate their goals. This process is important not only for individual achievement but also for developing an atmosphere of tolerance. Understanding that all people share basic interests and face similar fears and challenges will lead students to a deeper understanding of other people and their motives. The chapter is divided into two sections: the first five lessons help students articulate their interests and the last four teach them the process of setting goals.

SESSIONS

INTERESTS AND SKILLS

Life Skills

Our Interests

Steps to Understanding

Life's River

Challenges

SETTING GOALS

Creating the Future

Focusing on the Goal

Aiming for the Goal

Trajectory of Success

LIFE SKILLS

This lesson helps students understand that they need certain skills in order to be socially responsible individuals. Acquiring these skills is a key step toward tolerance.

OBJECTIVES

Upon completing this lesson, the students will have learned about the cultures and customs of various ethnic groups and their contributions to society.

MATERIALS NEEDED

Small pieces of yellow paper and pink paper (enough so that each student has one piece of each color. You may use two other colors of your choice.)
Tape

TEACHER TIPS

Remember to point out that all the skills the students offer illustrate the strength of diversity.

OPENING QUESTIONS

1. Can you build a home without skills?
2. Can one achieve a goal without skills?
3. Can you be a responsible member of society without skills?

ACTIVITY

1. Give each student a piece of pink paper and a piece of yellow paper.
2. Tell them to write "I am looking for" on the yellow paper and indicate a particular life skill they want to master. Ask them to write "I offer" on the pink piece and indicate what life skill they have to offer.
3. Draw two columns on the chalkboard. Label one "I am looking for" and the other "I offer." Ask the students to tape their pieces of paper to the appropriate column. If they find a similar statement, they are to tape their paper over it.

4. Once all students have taped their requests and offers, ask the class to review the master list and determine what are the most required and most offered skills. Discuss the results with the class.

DISCUSSION QUESTIONS

1. What life skills do you need to determine your life goals?
2. What skills do you need to achieve your goals?
3. What skills do you need to overcome barriers to your goals?

OUR INTERESTS

Defining personal and common interests is a key element of this curriculum. Students may not initially understand the relationship between their interests and tolerance, but that relationship is close. Competing interests lead to conflict and intolerance; common interests lead to collaboration and tolerance. Understanding the interests all people share will help the students develop tolerance.

OBJECTIVES

Upon completing this lesson, the students will have learned that understanding their interests and those of others is necessary for creating tolerance.

MATERIALS NEEDED

My Main Interests activity sheet (copy for each student)
Portrait of Interests activity sheet (copy for each student)

OPENING QUESTIONS

1. Why do we try to achieve goals?
2. What kind of life do we consider valuable?
3. What are the valuable elements of life?

ACTIVITY

Part 1: My Interests

1. Ask the students to complete My Main Interests activity sheet.
2. Once the class has completed the assignment, lead the students in a discussion of individual and common interests based on the results of the activity sheets.

Part 2: Portrait of Interests

1. Distribute Portrait of Interests activity sheet and tell the students to list as many answers to the questions as they can.

2. Draw three columns on the board. Label them "I," "Others," and "Common." Have the class compile a master list of "I" and "Others" from their activity sheets.
3. Ask the class to evaluate the importance of each item and rank the items in each column.
4. Ask the class to compare the two lists. Do any items appear on both? Write these under "Common." Ask if any of the items that appeared in both columns are of similar rank. Tell the class that they have now created a "Portrait of Interests."

DISCUSSION QUESTIONS

1. Would we aspire to goals if we didn't have interests?
2. Can we encourage someone's interests without having interests of our own?

Activity Sheet

My Main Interests

Instructions: Choose 10 items that you consider most important to you.

- Acquisition of practical skills
- Appearance
- Being needed
- Career
- Cheerful attitude toward life
- Communication and understanding
- Culture (arts, etc.)
- Education
- Family
- Friends
- Getting to know myself
- Getting to know others
- Health
- Helping the world
- Leadership
- Life experience
- Money
- Personal achievement
- Public recognition
- Relationships with important or famous people
- Respect
- Self-reliance
- Spiritual values
- Status

Activity Sheet

Portrait of Interests

I	Others
What do I want most? ______ ______ ______ ______ ______	What do others want most? ______ ______ ______ ______ ______
Why am I interesting to others? ______ ______ ______ ______ ______	Why are others interesting to me? ______ ______ ______ ______ ______
What do I want to achieve ______ ______ ______ ______ ______	What do others want to achieve? ______ ______ ______ ______ ______
What will I fight for? ______ ______ ______ ______ ______	What will others fight for? ______ ______ ______ ______ ______

STEPS TO UNDERSTANDING

Humans operate in a social environment in which people's interests and aspirations frequently clash. These clashes can lead to progress, but they can also lead to conflict because people do not realize the constraints under which others operate, and they do not understand that helping others improve their lives and achieve their goals will help society at large. In this exercise students learn that people's situations may limit their ability to live life fully and may lead to frustrations that can result in intolerance.

OBJECTIVES

Upon completing this lesson, the students will be able to do the following:

1. Understand that people's life situation can lead to frustration that breeds intolerance
2. Understand that helping others improve their lives improves everyone's life and leads to tolerance

MATERIALS NEEDED

A Step Forward! teacher resource sheet

PREPARATION

Cut out each role in A Step Forward! teacher resource sheet or write each on a small index card or piece of paper. Adjust the list for the number of students in the class. Make sure to include a variety of occupations with a wide variety of salaries.

OPENING QUESTIONS

1. Can we achieve our personal goals if other people do not achieve theirs?
2. Can society achieve its goals if individuals do not achieve theirs?

ACTIVITY

1. Give each student an index card with a role and ask the class to form a "starting line." Tell the students to hold their cards in front of them during the exercise.
2. Tell the students that they are to move forward a step if they can answer "Yes" to a question you will ask.

3. Read each question on A Step Forward! teacher resource sheet and pause before each so the students can consider their answer and move forward, if possible.
4. After you have asked all the questions, tell the class to look at the position of various members. Have all reached the “finish line”? Who is farthest from the finish line? Is there a pattern among those who have not reached it?
5. Ask each student to describe how he feels about his position with respect to the finish line.
6. Ask the students what conclusions they can draw from the activity and from their feelings about their position.

Teacher Resource Sheet

A Step Forward!

Roles

Write each role on an index card or a small piece of paper. Adjust the list for the number of students in the class.

Artist
Assembly line worker
Bank executive
Cashier in a food store
Chief executive officer of large company
Clerk in a department store
Construction worker
Doctor
Engineer
Farmer
Housewife
Journalist
Lawyer
Maid
Mechanic
Musician in a symphony orchestra
Nanny
Police officer
Pop music star
Professional baseball player
Salesman
Scientist
Secretary
Student in Africa
Student in the United States
Teacher
University professor
Unskilled laborer
Writer

Questions

1. Can you afford going to the movies and theater often?
2. Do you have enough pocket money?
3. Can you buy a completely new wardrobe every season?
4. Can you afford to buy a new car?
5. Do you take a vacation every summer?
6. Can you live on your income?
7. Do you pay all your bills on time?
8. Can you afford to give expensive gifts to your friends?
9. Can you go to a good restaurant more than once a month?
10. Can you afford to renovate your home?
11. Can you afford a spa treatment?
12. Can you buy everything that you want?
13. Do you have state-of-the-art electronic equipment in your house?
14. Can you afford to buy an apartment or a house?
15. Can you afford to visit any country you wish?

LIFE'S RIVER

One of the major steps in learning life skills and developing tolerance is understanding that all lives have both good and bad times from which we can gain wisdom. Using the metaphors of a river and a map helps the students understand that that they will face good and bad times and that all people have similar experiences and mutual interests.

OBJECTIVES

Upon completing this lesson, the students will be able to understand some of the experiences they have had and the challenges they will encounter in their lives and to relate those experiences and challenges to the lives of others.

MATERIALS NEEDED

Drawing paper
Colored pencils or crayons

OPENING QUESTIONS

1. Have you ever taken an interesting trip?
2. What made it interesting?

ACTIVITY

1. Ask the students to define *metaphor*. Tell them that they are going to draw a picture of a mountain river that will be a metaphor for their journey through life.
2. Tell the students that their river should have islands, underwater rocks, coves, and rapids, and that their picture should include a house and beautiful scenery. Ask them what they think each element in their picture symbolizes in their life. Remind them to include the water!
3. Ask the students to note experiences from their real life under each element. For example, under "rapids" they might note a time in their life when they felt out of control.
4. Ask student volunteers to present their pictures and discuss with the class. Lead the discussion to the common experiences presented under the elements to show what all people have in common.

5. Tell the students that the pictures they drew were of the course of an individual life. They can draw the course of many lives by using a map as a metaphor. Ask them to brainstorm how they would do this. What would symbolize hard times? Challenges? Conflicts among individuals? Cooperation among individuals?
6. Based on their thoughts, have them create the map.

DISCUSSION QUESTIONS

1. How does the water in the river affect its surroundings?
2. How do the elements in or near the river affect the course of the water?
3. From which points in your "river" do you get the best perspectives on life?
4. What does this tell you about your life's journey?
5. How can you relate the metaphor of the river to tolerance?

CHALLENGES

In this session students are asked not to think about abstract problems but about the real problems that they, their friends, and their community face. They will discuss why these situations can cause conflict and lead to intolerance, and brainstorm some concrete suggestions for solving the problems. This session is a key element in this course because it presents real issues that the students can address in future lessons.

OBJECTIVES

Upon completing this lesson, students will be able to articulate the challenges they face in their personal lives, school, and community.

MATERIALS NEEDED

Challenges activity sheet (copy for each student)

TEACHER TIPS

You will find this an enlightening exercise because it gives you the opportunity to view problems through other people's eyes.

Students may want to amend their list as the course progresses.

OPENING QUESTIONS

1. Have you ever been challenged? In what way?
2. Have you ever challenged someone? In what way?
3. Have you ever challenged yourself? In what way?

ACTIVITY

1. Divide the board into four columns labeled "Town," "School," "Family," and "Personal." Ask the students to list what they think are the main challenges for each group in the appropriate column.
2. Ask the students to share their suggestions and to justify each. Create a class master list for each category. (The class list should include no more than 15 problems in each category.)

3. Ask the class to vote for the three most important problems in each category and to explain their choices. Tell them to write the challenge in each of the appropriate columns and save the activity sheet.

DISCUSSION QUESTIONS

1. What conclusions can you draw from the results of the exercises?
2. What is the main challenge we face in life?
3. Which of your personal problems do you consider most important?

ADDITIONAL ACTIVITY

Ask the class to imagine that they are knights and must open one of three doors in the castle. The sign on one door says, "You acquire knowledge, but you lose wealth." The sign on the second door says, "You get rich, but you lose your friends." The sign on the third says, "You win glory but lose love." Ask them to answer the following questions:

- Which door would you open?
- What would await you beyond the door?
- What will be your "armor," "weapons," and other resources?
- Where will you get them?

Activity Sheet

Challenges

Instructions: List the main challenges for each group in the appropriate column.

MAIN CHALLENGES

Town	School	Family	Personal
1.			
2.			
3.			
4.			
5.			

Instructions: Record the three challenges the class has determined are most important for each category in the appropriate column below.

Town	School	Family	Personal
1.			
2.			
3.			

CREATING THE FUTURE

Humans continually think about the future and model their actions on the future they dream of. Thus, they are the only creatures capable of creating their future. In this lesson, the students will learn how to visualize their future as the first step in making their dreams a reality.

OBJECTIVES

Upon completing this lesson, the students will have a way of visualizing how they approach the future.

MATERIALS NEEDED

Five Methods of Visualizing the Future activity sheet (copy for each student)

OPENING QUESTIONS

1. What do you daydream about?
2. What do people get from dreaming?
3. Does the present create the future or does the future create the present?

ACTIVITY

1. Tell the students that there are five ways of visualizing how we look at the future:

   The Pinocchio Method: imagining the future from what we see today

   The Shakespeare Method: embracing life as an evolving drama over which we have little control

   The Jules Verne Method: creating the future based on a well laid out course

   The Don Quixote Method: striving to reach impossible goals

   The Blue Caterpillar Method: growing the future from within

2. Ask the class to form groups based on their preferred method. Ask each group to develop a short play that illustrates the distinctive features of their method and shows the advantages of using the method in dealing with the future.
3. Have each group stage its play. Once the presentations are complete, ask the class to evaluate the advantages and disadvantages of each method. At the end of the discussion, remind the students that no one method is better than another. The important thing to remember is that people have a way of making their own future.

4. End the session by telling the students:

    Each of us already has our own future: Hear it.

    Each of us has our own path toward the future: See it.

    You are on the trajectory to the future: Do not hold back.

DISCUSSION QUESTIONS

1. Why is visualizing your future important?
2. Some of the methods for visualizing the future are based on setting impossible goals or on viewing life as not under the individual's complete control. Are these methods valid? Why or why not?

ACTIVITY SHEET

FIVE METHODS OF VISUALIZING THE FUTURE

The Pinocchio Method: imagining the future from what we see today

The Shakespeare Method: embracing life as a evolving drama over which we have no control

The Jules Verne Method: creating the future based on a well laid out course

The Don Quixote Method: striving to reach impossible goals

The Blue Caterpillar Method: growing the future from within

Instructions:
Determine your group's method of visualizing the future and list its advantages and disadvantages.

My Group's Method:______________________________

Advantages	Disadvantages
1.	1.
2.	2.
3.	3.
4.	4.
5.	5.

FOCUSING ON THE GOAL

Humans are the only creatures who can transform their desires into conscious goals. This exercise is designed to help students become aware that setting goals is a deliberate process that can involve numerous steps. It also teaches them that goals must be concrete, based in reality and on their interests.

OBJECTIVES

Upon completing this lesson, students will be able to accomplish the following:

1. Set goals
2. Understand the importance of focusing on a goal

MATERIALS NEEDED

Focusing on a Goal activity sheet (copy for each student)

TEACHER TIPS

Many teenagers do not yet have life goals, or their goals may be unrealistic. Assure the students that it is okay if they are unsure of their goal. The purpose of this exercise is not to set definite goals but to begin the process of thinking about realistic goals.

OPENING QUESTIONS

1. Why are goals important?
2. Is a goal the same as a dream?

ACTIVITY

1. Remind the students of the definition of *metaphor*.
2. Tell the students that the class will explore how to work toward a goal by using the metaphor of a ship navigating a dangerous channel to reach its home port.
3. The ship has a navigator and a captain. Ask the class to define the duties of each. Explain that the navigator knows where the rocks, shoals, and dangerous currents are and where the water is deep and safe. He recommends the course to the captain, who determines whether to accept his recommendation and who is responsible for guiding the ship.

4. Tell the students that we need to act like navigators and captains to achieve our goals. We need to be captains to guide the ship of our life to reach our goal. We need to be navigators to find the best course toward our goal and to keep us from wandering off course or from "colliding" with others.
5. Distribute Focusing on a Goal activity sheet. Ask the students to be the captain and list one goal for each category. Then tell the students to act as the navigator and think of the possible courses they could take to reach the goal. Ask them to list any obstacles that they think they will encounter as well as the advantages of each course. Ask them to again become the captain and choose the best course to reach their goal.

DISCUSSION QUESTIONS

1. Do we always encounter barriers when working toward a goal?
2. Is the shortest way to a goal always the best?
3. Is there only one right way to achieve a goal?

Activity Sheet

Focusing on a Goal

Short-term goal

Possible Courses	Obstacles	Advantages
1.	1.	1.
2.	2.	2.
3.	3.	3.

Long-term goal

Possible Courses	Obstacles	Advantages
1.	1.	1.
2.	2.	2.
3.	3.	3.

Life goal

Possible Courses	Obstacles	Advantages
1.	1.	1.
2.	2.	2.
3.	3.	3.

AIMING FOR THE GOAL

Teenagers often set goals without knowing how to attain them. We can teach them how to clarify their goals and outline the steps needed to achieve them, but first students must learn that they need the will and spirit to work toward what they want. Self-motivation is essential for achievement.

OBJECTIVES

Upon completing this lesson, students will understand that self-motivation is needed to achieve a goal.

MATERIALS NEEDED

Aiming for the Goal activity sheet (copy for each student)
Poster board (optional)

OPENING QUESTIONS

Was there ever a situation when you really, really wanted something—you absolutely had to have it? What did you feel like? How did you act?

ACTIVITY

1. Tell the students that reaching for a goal is like an archer launching an arrow toward a target. He carefully chooses his strongest bow and fastest arrow and concentrates all his energy on aiming for his target.
2. Distribute Aiming for the Goal activity sheet and ask the students to complete the questionnaire.
3. Once the students have completed the assignment, organize the class into small groups. Tell each group to discuss the individual answers and develop a group answer to each question.
4. Ask each group to present its answers to the class.

DISCUSSION QUESTIONS

1. How do you transform a dream into a goal?
2. How do you begin striving for a goal?
3. From where do you get the energy and enthusiasm needed to achieve a goal?

ADDITIONAL ACTIVITY

1. Ask the students to develop mottoes or slogans that reflect the spirit needed to achieve goals.
2. Organize the class into a circle and ask the students to present their mottoes in a tone that reflects the energy needed to achieve goals.
3. List all the mottoes on a piece of poster board and tack it to the bulletin board so that the students can refer to it throughout the course.

Activity Sheet

Aiming for the Goal

1. What qualities do you need to achieve a goal?

2. Why do some people have goals while others do not?

3. What makes a goal all-encompassing? What kind of goal makes people forget about everything else in order to achieve it?

4. Why do people lack the will to work toward goals? Why does this lack affect so many people?

5. How can you encourage a person to aspire?

TRAJECTORY OF SUCCESS

This exercise creates a visual image of how people reach goals. Students will analyze three ways of working toward goals and focus on the importance of developing an overarching strategy when setting out to achieve a goal.

OBJECTIVES

Upon completing this lesson, students will learn the importance of developing strategies for achieving a goal.

MATERIALS NEEDED

Stairway to the Sky activity sheet (copy for each student)
Strategy activity sheet (copy for each student)

TEACHER TIPS

You could also begin this activity by asking the students to form a "starting line" and, on command, jump forward with both feet. Tell them to mark how far they got. Now tell them to return to the starting line, take one step forward on command, and mark how far they got. Ask the students how far they could get in a day using each method. Which is the most efficient way of traveling?

OPENING QUESTION

What is the meaning of the old Chinese proverb *A journey of 1,000 miles starts with one step?*

ACTIVITY

Part 1: Stairway to the Sky

1. Distribute Stairway to the Sky activity sheet. Ask the students how the picture describes two ways of working toward the goal. Ask them what each element of the picture stands for.

   Amoeba: the current situation

   Sun: the goal

   Large stairs: reaching for a goal through use of an overall strategy broken down into individual steps

Small steps: reaching for a goal by small steps without an overarching strategy

Rocket: targeting a goal in one step

2. Ask the students if one representation of working toward a goal is more realistic than the others? More efficient? Better? Tell them to write the benefits and drawbacks of each representation on the activity sheet.
3. Ask volunteers to share their thoughts with the class. Guide the discussion so that the students understand that although people can work toward goals in many ways (based on personality and preference), one of the most effective is to develop a strategy and then work in steps.

Part 2: Strategies

1. Distribute Strategy activity sheet. Explain that developing a strategy has the following elements:
   - Determining priorities
   - Developing steps based on priorities
   - Determining the way or ways to execute each step
   - Determining the resources needed for each step
   - Determining ways to evaluate the success of each step
   - Revising the steps or strategy as needed
2. Ask the students to decide on a goal (it doesn't have to be realistic) and develop a strategy for reaching it.
3. Ask volunteers to share their strategies.

Activity Sheet

Stairway to the Sky

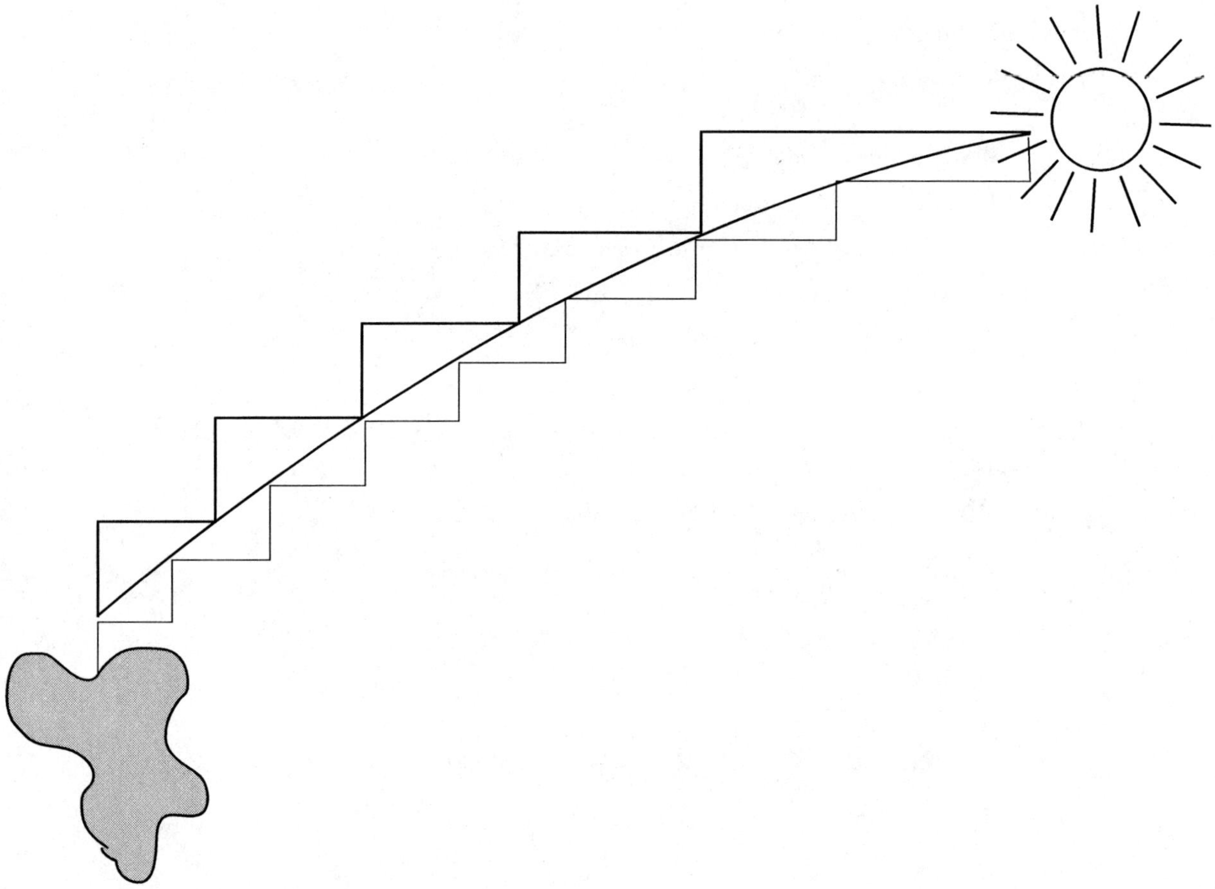

Way 1: ____

Benefits	Drawbacks
1.	1.
2.	2.
3.	3.
4.	4.
5.	5.

Way 2: ____

Benefits	Drawbacks
1.	1.
2.	2.
3.	3.
4.	4.
5.	5.

Strategy

Elements of a Strategy

1. **Determine priorities.**

2. **Develop steps based on priorities.**

3. **Determine the way or ways to execute each step.**

4. **Determine the resources needed for each step.**

5. **Determine ways to evaluate the success of each step.**

6. **Revise the steps or strategy as needed.**

Instructions: Set a goal (it does not have to be realistic). Use the elements above to develop a strategy for reaching a goal and outline the strategy below.

Chapter 4
POSSIBILITIES AND CHALLENGES

Chapter 4 helps students understand their possibilities, determine the resources they have to achieve their goals, and understand and deal with the challenges they will face in life. It continues the theme of Chapter 3—that all people have similar experiences and understanding these experiences will build tolerance. The first five lessons help students realistically assess their possibilities and discover the resources around them—particularly people—that will help them achieve their goals. The last six lessons help them see and deal with challenges in a positive manner.

Sessions

POSSIBILITIES AND RESOURCES

- Beginning from a Blank Sheet
- Our Possibilities
- Answers
- Resources Around Us
- Hidden Resources

OVERCOMING CHALLENGES

- The Road to a Goal
- What Hampers Achievement?
- The Value of Obstacles
- Two Models
- Start with Yourself
- Visualizing Success

BEGINNING FROM A BLANK SHEET

Teenagers often lack self-confidence. They fear that they do not have the abilities or skills they need to succeed in life. This lesson will teach them that they can succeed because visualizing the future is the first step in making it become a reality.

OBJECTIVES

Upon completing this lesson, students will understand that they have the ability to shape their future.

MATERIALS NEEDED

Blank sheet of drawing paper for each student

TEACHER TIPS

The students may be self-conscious about their artwork. Ask for volunteers to begin the presentations. Remind the students to respect each other's work. This exercise is not about their ability to draw!

OPENING QUESTION

What do we mean when we say, "The future is in your hands"?

ACTIVITY

1. Give each student a blank piece of paper. Tell the students that the paper is their future. Ask them to create their future as they want to see it.
2. Do not give them any clues about how to create it. If they ask questions, such as, "May I use a ruler?" answer only, "Yes." If one student tries to imitate another, tell her that she has her own future and so cannot use another's.
3. Ask the students to present their futures. Are there any common themes?

DISCUSSION QUESTIONS

1. What does "if you can see it, you can do it" mean? How is this related to planning for the future?
2. How has hearing other students discuss their future helped you clarify your future?

OUR POSSIBILITIES

Teenagers frequently dream about their goals but do not think about the concrete steps needed to achieve them. One of the first steps is analyzing possibilities based on resources. This lesson helps students understand the importance of being realistic about the resources they have.

OBJECTIVES

Upon completing this lesson, students will be able to determine the most important resources they have to achieve their goals.

MATERIALS NEEDED

My Company Resources activity sheet (copy for each student)

OPENING QUESTIONS

1. From where do we get the things we need to achieve our goals?
2. Explain the following quote: "Whoever aspires searches for possibilities, whoever doesn't aspire searches for excuses."

ACTIVITY

1. Explain to the class that they are again going to use an analogy to understand one step in achieving goals: analyzing possibilities. In this case the analogy is of a major energy company searching for oil deposits. The company employs scientists who analyze geological maps and other data to determine where oil may lie, and then sends out explorers to test the scientists' theories. We are the company looking for the resources we need to achieve our goals. Our "scientists" determine where we might find these resources and our "explorers" see if these are really available.
2. Distribute My Company Resources activity sheet. Tell the students to review the resources listed and add any others they may think of.
3. Tell them to list their 10 most important resources. They can be from any category.
4. Once the students have completed the assignment, ask volunteers to share their resources. Determine if many in the class chose similar resources. If so, ask the students why they considered them important.

Activity Sheet

My Company Resources

Emotional
Enthusiasm
Ambition
Determination
Interest
Positive outlook

Financial
Personal
Family and relatives
Scholarships and grants

Informational
Internet and other electronic resources
Libraries
Mentors

Intellectual
Knowledge
Talents
Ideas
Creativity
Intuition

Material
Computer
Phone
Other equipment

Societal
Friends
Family
Contacts

Instructions: List the top 10 resources you have to achieve your goals. Make sure they are based on reality.

1. ______________________________

2. ______________________________

3. ______________________________

4. ______________________________

5. ______________________________

6. ______________________________

7. ______________________________

8. ______________________________

9. ______________________________

10. ______________________________

ANSWERS

The exercise is designed to give students a dynamic image of how they can search for ways to overcome obstacles, solve problems, and achieve their desired goals. By exploring the metaphor of Theseus and the Labyrinth, they will come to understand the importance of developing the ability to find and use resources—including other people—to achieve personal goals.

OBJECTIVES

Upon completing this lesson, the students will understand the following:

1. The importance of finding and using recourses to solve problems
2. Other people and their skills are important resources

MATERIALS NEEDED

Labyrinth activity sheet (copy for each student)

TEACHER TIPS

You can find the story of Theseus and the Labyrinth at http://www.explorecrete.com/history/labyrinth-minotaur.htm

OPENING QUESTION

Why have people set out on hazardous missions?

ACTIVITY

1. Tell the class the story of Theseus and the Labyrinth. Remember to include Ariadne's thread. Remind the students of the definition of *metaphor* and tell them that the story of Theseus conquering the Labyrinth is a metaphor for solving life's problems and challenges.
2. Explain that the class will explore three labyrinths—the challenges they face as
    - individuals,
    - family members,
    - members of society.

Divide the class into three groups, distribute Labyrinth activity sheet, and assign each group a labyrinth.

3. Tell the groups that before they begin their exploration, each group must determine the seven most important resources they will need. What will they need to solve problems, overcome obstacles, and achieve their goals? What will be "Ariadne's thread," the thread that enables them to navigate the labyrinth and get out safely? Tell them to write these resources on the activity sheet.
4. Once the groups have completed the sheets, ask each to present its findings to the entire class. Ask the students if there are common skills needed to navigate each labyrinth.
5. Lead a discussion of the importance of finding and using resources in solving life's problems. Stress that in today's society resources are not necessarily objects. They also include other people with different skills.
6. Summarize the theme of this session.

   There are two ways to achieve goals:

   • Through selfish individual action, aggression, and violence: INTOLERANCE

   • Through mutual understanding, collaboration, and respect: TOLERANCE

DISCUSSION QUESTIONS

1. Why is it important to work together to achieve goals?
2. How is the acquisition of life skills, such as the ability to find and use resources, related to tolerance?

Activity Sheet

Labyrinth

LABYRINTH:____________________________________

Seven Important Resources:

1. ____________________________________

2. ____________________________________

3. ____________________________________

4. ____________________________________

5. ____________________________________

6. ____________________________________

7. ____________________________________

Ariadne's Thread:

RESOURCES AROUND US

This activity continues the theme that students must actively search for the resources they need to achieve their goals and that the search must be grounded in reality. It teaches them that they frequently do not have to look very far—much of what they need may be around them.

OBJECTIVES

Upon completing this lesson, the students will be able to identify the resources around them that they can use to achieve their goals.

MATERIALS NEEDED

Resources Around Us activity sheet (copy for each student)

OPENING QUESTION

Why do people sometimes not see what is in front of them?

ACTIVITY

1. Tell the students that when trying to achieve a goal people often fail to notice the resources they have around them.
2. Divide the class into three groups. The first is to brainstorm the resources available in the family, the second the resources in the school, and the third the resources in the town or city. Have each group present and explain its results.
3. Distribute Resources Around Us activity sheet. Ask the class to compile a master list of resources and vote for the five most important in each category. Have the students enter these on their activity sheets.
4. Tell the students that the resources they just listed are available to everyone in the class. Ask the students to think of the resources in each category that are specific to them as individuals, and enter them in the activity sheet.

DISCUSSION QUESTIONS

1. Why should you evaluate the resources available before starting a project?
2. Why is it important to look specifically for those around you?
3. What was the most difficult aspect of evaluating your resources?

Activity Sheet

Resources Around Us

FIVE IMPORTANT RESOURCES AROUND US

Family	School	City
1.		
2.		
3.		
4.		
5.		

FIVE IMPORTANT RESOURCES AROUND ME

Family	School	City
1.		
2.		
3.		
4.		
5.		

HIDDEN RESOURCES

This lesson connects personal achievement with tolerance by teaching students the power of collaboration and the importance of understanding the capabilities of others.

OBJECTIVES

Upon completing this lesson, the students will understand that they can best develop their potential by working with others.

MATERIALS NEEDED

My Partner's Treasures activity sheet (copy for each student)

OPENING QUESTIONS

1. What to people mean when they say that "it was hidden in plain sight"?
2. Do you think any of your resources are hidden this way?

ACTIVITY

1. Tell the students that, as they have learned, they cannot reach their goals by themselves. They need the help of other people. In this exercise they will work in pairs to find the "hidden treasure," the hidden capacities of their partners.
2. Divide the group into pairs and distribute My Partner's Treasures activity sheet. Tell the students to find three important qualities or capabilities their partners have that will help them achieve their goals. They can use any method they want—interview, intuition, etc. Tell them to write the "treasures" on the sheet.
3. Tell each student to list the ways she used to find her partner's treasures on the activity sheet.
4. Tell the students to give their activity sheets to their partners so the partners have a list of their own treasures and suggestions about ways to find their own capabilities.
5. Assemble the class and lead a discussion of the activity. Ask for volunteers to discuss the treasures they found. Are there some that most students have in common?
6. Ask the students to evaluate the methods they used to find the treasures.

DISCUSSION QUESTIONS

1. Are some ways of finding your capabilities better or more efficient than others? Who else might you consult to discover your hidden treasures?
2. How is tolerant collaboration important in achieving your potential?

Activity Sheet

My Partner's Treasures

Three Treasures

1.

2.

3.

How I Found Your Treasures

1.

2.

3.

THE ROAD TO A GOAL

Achieving a goal involves not only moving toward it but also exercising caution and avoiding the hazards along the way. This lesson helps students explore those cautions and hazards while developing "rules of the road" for working toward a goal.

OBJECTIVES

Upon completing this lesson, students will understand the rules, cautions, and hazards they must address when working toward a goal.

MATERIALS NEEDED

Road to a Goal activity sheet (copy for each student)

OPENING QUESTION

When can a curved road be quicker to a destination than a straight one?

ACTIVITY

1. Tell the students that moving toward a goal is like taking a car trip. You must choose your route. Then, you must obey the rules of the road and watch for road signs signaling caution or hazard along the route.
2. Divide the class into three groups. Ask each group to explain how one part of the road trip relates to achieving a goal:

    Group A: rules of the road

    Group B: signs indicating caution (aspects of their journey they must pay close attention to)

    Group C: signs indicating road hazards (situations they must avoid)
3. Ask each group to present its thoughts. Discuss the presentations with the entire class.
4. Reassemble the groups. Ask Group A to develop rules of the road for working toward a goal. Tell Group B to suggest situations that require caution—paying close attention—as it moves toward a goal. Ask Group C to think of hazardous situations along the route to a goal.
5. Ask each group to present its thoughts. Distribute Road to a Goal activity sheet and discuss the presentations with the entire class. Have the students write a master list of rules and signs on their sheets.

DISCUSSION QUESTIONS

1. What makes the road to a goal longer? Shorter?
2. Is the safest road always the best?
3. How do you choose a road through life that offers the best opportunities for achieving your goal?

Activity Sheet

Road to a Goal

Rules of the Road	Situations Requiring Caution	Hazardous Situations
1.		
2.		
3.		
4.		
5.		

WHAT HAMPERS ACHIEVEMENT?

Before the students can work toward their goals, they have to understand the factors that might hold them back. This lesson helps them analyze both the external (lack of education or finances, etc.) and internal (lack of motivation or their own fears, etc.) obstacles to success. By determining not only their own obstacles but those of their friends, they begin to look beyond themselves. They develop an understanding of another person and learn that all people face the same kinds of obstacles. This knowledge is key to developing tolerance.

OBJECTIVES

Upon completing this lesson, students will be able to articulate their internal and external barriers to success.

MATERIALS NEEDED

Obstacles activity sheet (copy for each student)
2 blank sheets of paper for each student

OPENING QUESTIONS

1. Why do some very smart people never achieve their goals?
2. How do we react to obstacles?

ACTIVITY

1. Distribute the blank sheets of paper. Ask each student to draw a picture of one of the main obstacles he faces in achieving his personal goals. This can be internal or external. The students can use any technique they like. The drawing can be representational, symbolic, abstract, etc.
2. Now, ask each student to use the second sheet to draw a picture of an important obstacle he thinks a friend faces. He should not name his friend or show him the drawing. Tell each student to compare his two drawings. Do they have anything in common?
3. Ask volunteers to describe their drawings and explain how they chose their obstacles. As they do so, list the obstacles on the board.
4. Distribute Obstacles activity sheet and draw two columns on the board. Label one column "External Obstacles" and the other "Internal Obstacles." Ask the class to determine the 10 most important obstacles and ask them to indicate whether it is an internal or external ob-

stacle. Tell them to write the obstacle in the appropriate column on the activity sheet while you write it in the column on the board.

5. Ask the class how they might address the obstacles. Are there some obstacles they must overcome? Are there some they can avoid? Tell them to write an "O" next to those they must overcome and an "A" next to those they can avoid.
6. Lead a discussion of their attitude toward obstacles, focusing on the importance of dealing with their fears of the obstacles they face.

DISCUSSION QUESTIONS

1. Why do some people see possibilities while others see only barriers?
2. What role does fear play in preventing us from achieving our goals?
3. Of what are we most afraid?
4. Is there anything positive about fear?
5. What hinders people more, themselves or their circumstances?

ACTIVITY SHEET

OBSTACLES

Instructions:

1. List the 10 most important obstacles in the appropriate column.
2. Place an "O" next to it if you must overcome the obstacle. Place an "A" next to it if you might be able avoid it.

Internal Obstacles	O/A	External Obstacles	O/A

THE VALUE OF OBSTACLES

Teenagers often view obstacles as barriers. They perceive them as difficulties and dangers. This lesson teaches them to think positively about obstacles so that they can view them as possibilities.

OBJECTIVES

Upon completing this lesson, the students will understand the value of obstacles.

MATERIALS NEEDED

Value of Obstacles activity sheet (copy for each student)
Completed Challenges activity sheet (page 85)

TEACHER TIPS

It may be difficult for students to think of the benefits of obstacles. Here are a few:

- Discovering personal possibilities and capabilities
- Cultivating new experiences, knowledge, and skills
- Encouraging collaboration
- Encouraging creativity
- Gaining an understanding of others
- Experiencing the joy of overcoming challenges

OPENING QUESTION

Can good things ever come from bad experiences?

ACTIVITY

1. Distribute Value of Obstacles activity sheet and ask the students to complete it.
2. Once they have completed the assignment, conduct a general discussion of the positive and negative sides of obstacles.
3. Ask them to review their completed Challenges activity sheet and to brainstorm the positive elements in the challenges they listed. Tell them to add these to their activity sheet.

DISCUSSION QUESTIONS

1. What role do obstacles play in our lives?
2. Can obstacles contribute to tolerance? How?

Activity Sheet

Value of Obstacles

Part 1:

Instructions: List the positive and negative sides of obstacles in the table below.

Positive	Negative
1.	
2.	
3.	
4.	
5.	

Part 2:

Instructions: List the three most important challenges for each category (from Challenges session) in the first column. Write the positive elements of each in the second.

Major Challenge	**Positive Element**
TOWN: 1. 2. 3.	TOWN: 1. 2. 3.
SCHOOL: 1. 2. 3.	SCHOOL: 1. 2. 3.
FAMILY: 1. 2. 3.	FAMILY: 1. 2. 3.
PERSONAL: 1. 2. 3.	PERSONAL: 1. 2. 3.

TWO MODELS

Our basic attitudes can affect how we progress toward our goals. We can look at the changes we need to make and the challenges we face either negatively or positively. We can say, "No! I'm opposed!!!" or we can say, "Yes! I'm for it!!!" We can work for something or against it; we can fight for what we want or we can fight against what we don't want. In this lesson, students learn that a negative attitude leads to conflict, blocks creativity, and impedes their progress. A positive attitude engenders self-confidence, encourages resourcefulness, and helps students achieve their goals efficiently. They will discover that a negative attitude can lead to frustration, aggression, and intolerance, while a positive attitude can lead to adaptation, acceptance, and tolerance.

OBJECTIVES

Upon completing this lesson, students will learn the importance of a positive attitude in achieving their goals and working toward tolerance.

MATERIALS NEEDED

Two Models activity sheet (copy for each student)

TEACHER TIPS

You may want to extend this lesson by discussing the items the students listed in each column. Realizing that they have much in common will help students develop tolerance.

OPENING QUESTIONS

1. How do you feel when you are asked to make changes or encounter challenges?
2. How do you decide how to deal with them?

ACTIVITY

1. Distribute Two Models activity sheet and tell the students that there are two attitudes people can have in working toward their goals: positive or negative.

2. Tell the students to determine the three main things they want in their lives—what they ought to achieve, create, etc.—and write these in the column designated "I Want!"
3. Tell the students to determine the three most important things they don't want in their personal lives, family, school, society, etc., and write these in the column marked "I Don't Want!"
4. Tell the students to list the three most important things worth fighting for in their personal life, their family, and society, and enter them in the column labeled "For!"
5. Ask the students to list the three most important things they should fight against in their personal life, their family, and society, and write them in the column labeled "Against!"
6. Once the class has completed the assignment, ask them which model, the negative or the positive, was more difficult to use? Was more interesting and effective?
7. Ask the students how they can turn the negatives on their activity sheets into positives.

DISCUSSION QUESTIONS

1. How are people's attitudes toward challenges reflected in other areas of their life?
2. Which attitude is more likely to help develop tolerance?

Activity Sheet

Two Models

Instructions:

1. List the three main things you want in your life in the first column
2. List the three most important things you don't want in your personal life, family, school, society, etc. in the second column.
3. List the three most important things worth fighting for in your personal life, family, and society in the third column.
4. List the three most important things you should fight against in your personal life, family, and society in the fourth column.

I WANT!	I DON'T WANT!	FOR!	AGAINST!
1.			
2.			
3.			

START WITH YOURSELF

Some people fail not because of external circumstances but because of negative attitudes about themselves. In this session the students confront their own negative attitudes and learn thc value of replacing them with positive ones. Positive self-attitudes are important in building tolerance. Unless people learn to be tolerant of themselves, they cannot be tolerant of others.

OBJECTIVES

Upon completing this lesson, students will learn how to overcome their negative attitudes about themselves.

MATERIALS NEEDED

none

TEACHER TIPS

Make sure that the students understand that they should alter one negative quality at a time.

OPENING QUESTIONS

1. Would people who have a bad attitude about themselves ever want to succeed?
2. Can they succeed?

ACTIVITY

Part 1: My Personality

1. Ask the students to draw a tree that represents their personality.
2. Tell the students to alternately write a negative and a positive personality trait on the branches.
3. Ask the students to examine their tree. What branch would they cut first? Which branch would they grab first? What does the trunk symbolize?

Part 2: My Traits

1. Divide the class into small groups. Ask each group to think of four negative personality traits.
2. Have each group brainstorm how they would alter the traits so that they become positive and help the students achieve their goals.
3. Ask each group to report back to the class and have the class add their suggestions to each group's recommendations.

DISCUSSION QUESTIONS

1. What personal qualities stop you from achieving your goal?
2. How can you change these negative qualities into positives?

VISUALIZING SUCCESS

Often students feel paralyzed when they meet obstacles or experience failure. This exercise helps students remember how they felt when they achieved an important goal. By remembering how they felt when they were successful, they can use these visualizations whenever they need to become energized for success.

OBJECTIVES

Upon completing this lesson, students will have developed a personal vision of success.

MATERIALS NEEDED

none

TEACHER TIPS

Because students are visualizing very private moments, you should not ask them to share their experiences unless they choose to do so.

OPENING QUESTIONS

1. What does *visualization* mean?
2. Why do people use visualizations?

ACTIVITY

1. Ask the students to think of a very memorable moment in which they overcame an obstacle or achieved an important goal. Tell them that they are going to describe very specifically what they experienced.
2. Ask them to write down the smallest details of that experience that they can remember: the clothes they wore, the sounds they heard, the words people said, even the weather conditions.
3. Ask them to write down how they felt when they achieved success, for example, were they happy? Did they feel energized?

4. Explain to the students that they have now created their own visualization of what it feels to be successful. They can turn to this model to energize themselves when they need to overcome obstacles.
5. If students feel comfortable, ask for volunteers to share some of the feelings they experienced when they achieved a goal.

DISCUSSION QUESTIONS

1. Are there feelings common to all incidents of success?
2. How can visualizing success help us achieve our goals?

Chapter 5
COMMUNICATION

Chapter 5 teaches students the various means of communication and how to evaluate the effectiveness of each type. It also introduces them to important person-to-person skills and formal presentations. The chapter begins with an important session on listening and then investigates the limits of verbal and non-verbal communication. The next sessions ask students to explore how they perceive others and how others perceive them. Students are then asked to evaluate various forms of communication. The chapter ends with sessions on how to act when meeting individuals and how to conduct a win-win negotiation.

Sessions

Listening
Tell Me Clearly . . .
How Do People Perceive Us?
How Do We Perceive Others?
Communicate!
Get In Contact!
Negotiating

LISTENING

Teenagers often don't listen carefully. They become distracted by their surroundings or begin thinking of something else. They may think they have heard what another person has said and so jump to complete his sentences. This type of listening is merely rude in daily life, but it can cause serious problems in conflict situations, when people are too busy formulating their responses to listen attentively to their opponent. In contrast, a tolerant society practices active listening, a way of listening and responding to another person that improves mutual understanding. In this lesson, the students will learn what is involved in the process of active listening.

OBJECTIVES

Upon completing this lesson, students will understand the following:

1. The importance of good listening behavior
2. What constitutes good listening behavior

MATERIALS NEEDED

Listening resource sheet (copy for each student)

TEACHER TIPS

As an alternative to this exercise, you can select a willing volunteer to give a speech about herself. Arrange two chairs in front of the room and sit facing the student. As the student speaks, demonstrate bad listening behavior, then move to good listening behavior. Ask the class members for their reaction. Distribute Listening resource sheet and review.

OPENING QUESTION

How can you tell if someone is really listening?

ACTIVITY

1. Distribute Listening resource sheet and review.
2. Divide the class into pairs with the students facing their partners.

3. Give one member of each pair one minute to tell his partner the most important thing about himself. Meanwhile his partner is to listen using bad listening feedback. She is then to repeat what she has heard.
4. Ask the partner who discussed himself how he felt as he presented his important information. Ask the other member of the pair if she remembered the most important thing about her partner.
5. Repeat the exercise, but this time with the partner using good listening feedback.
6. Ask the partner who discussed himself how he felt as he presented his important information. Ask the other member of the pair if she remembered the most important thing about her partner.

DISCUSSION QUESTIONS

1. What other ways can you use to show people that you are interested in what they are saying?
2. Why is it important to repeat what someone is telling you?

Listening

Type Of Listening	Verbal Feedback	Non-verbal Feedback
Good	• Asks appropriate questions • Gives appropriate replies	• Sits attentively • Makes eye contact with speaker • Takes notes or otherwise indicates during conversation that she is listening
Bad	• Repeats questions that he has already asked or asks questions not connected to the discussion • Gives flippant replies	• Slouches or does not face speaker • Avoids eye contact • Looks bored or anxious to do something else

TELL ME CLEARLY

Because teenagers define communication as speaking or writing, they limit the ways they can express themselves and, consequently, the means available to them for achieving their goals. In this lesson they will learn that anything they do can carry information and that they can express their thoughts in many ways.

OBJECTIVES

Upon completing this lesson, the students will understand the types of messages they can communicate non-verbally.

MATERIALS NEEDED

None

OPENING QUESTIONS

1. Can you say something when you aren't talking?
2. Can we understand each other without saying a word?

ACTIVITIES

ACTIVITY 1: PASSING BUSES

1. Arrange the students into two parallel columns with the first student in one column facing the last student in the other. Explain that they are in buses going in opposite directions and that they have stopped side by side for exactly one minute.
2. Tell the students in the "first seats" of their buses that they must communicate something to each other but that they cannot speak. Give them exactly one minute.
3. After the time has elapsed, they must move to the rear of the bus so that the next pair of students can communicate something. Once they reach the rear of the bus, they can tell each other what they were trying to "say."
4. When everyone has communicated a message, ask the students if they had difficulty communicating without words. What does this exercise tell us about communicating with others?

ACTIVITY 2: TYPES OF NON-VERBAL INFORMATION

1. Divide the class into pairs. Give them a nonsense sentence and ask one member of each pair to express an emotion using the sentence. The partner is to guess the emotion.
2. Communicate to one member of each pair a feeling in terms of a color, smell, season of year, taste, weather, flower, etc. The partner has to guess the feeling.
3. Ask one member of each pair to draw an emotion. The partner is to guess what it is.
4. Ask one member of the pair to set the place and hour of an appointment without using words. Have the partner guess the place and hour.
5. Reassemble the group and lead a discussion about the types of information we can communicate non-verbally. Ask the class to brainstorm the possible types and write the list on the board.

DISCUSSION QUESTIONS

1. Why is it important to understand the types of non-verbal communication?
2. What information can you communicate non-verbally?
3. What are the benefits and drawbacks of communicating non-verbally?

HOW DO PEOPLE PERCEIVE US?

We work to achieve our goals with and among other people. These people perceive our views and deeds through the prism of their own personalities. In order to succeed, we must understand how they perceive us and must correct the misperceptions they may have. In this exercise, the students will learn how other people perceive them and discuss how they might change misperceptions.

OBJECTIVES

Upon completing this lesson, the students will understand the following:

1. How others perceive them
2. How they might change these perceptions

MATERIALS NEEDED

Drawing paper or blank paper
Colored pencils

TEACHER TIPS

As an alternative to this exercise, you can select a willing volunteer to give a speech about herself. Arrange two chairs in front of the room and sit facing the student. As the student speaks, demonstrate bad listening behavior, then move to good listening behavior. Ask the class members for their reaction. Distribute Listening resource sheet and review.

OPENING QUESTIONS

1. Is perception different from reality?
2. Have there been times when you perceived people or situations differently from what they really were?

ACTIVITY

Part 1: Portraits

1. Divide the class into pairs. Tell the students to draw pictures of their partners. The picture does not have to be a formal portrait. We don't care about the quality of the art! However,

along with a representation of the individual, the picture must be a "portrait" of the inner person—his interests, qualities, etc.

2. Have the students explain their portraits to their partners.
3. Ask the students to react to their portraits.
4. Reassemble the class. Lead discussions of how perception may differ from reality and how the students can change the way others see them.

Part 2: Telephone

1. Assemble the class in a circle and tell them that they are going to play a game of Telephone.
2. Whisper some problem in the ear of the student on your right. The student responds by saying, "If I understood you correctly, the problem is . . ." and then repeats your message.
3. Continue the game until each student has repeated the message.
4. Ask the last student who received the message to reveal it to the class. Is it different from the message you sent?
5. Lead a discussion of the effects of misinterpretation and how misinterpretation occurs.

DISCUSSION QUESTIONS

1. How do our self-perceptions differ from the perceptions others have of us?
2. What are the possible effects of misperceptions?
3. What can we do to change people's misperceptions of us?
4. Why is clear communication important?
5. What can we do to ensure clear communication?

HOW DO WE PERCEIVE OTHERS?

This lesson is an extension of the last session, in which the students discussed how others perceive them. Here they explore how they perceive others by investigating the importance of non-verbal communication.

OBJECTIVES

Upon completing this lesson, the student will accomplish the following:

1. Learn that our perception of others is based on both verbal and non-verbal communication
2. Understand the importance of non-verbal communication

MATERIALS NEEDED

Perceiving Others activity sheet (copy for each student)
Ten Rules for Perceiving Others activity sheet (copy for each student)

OPENING QUESTIONS

1. How do people communicate non-verbally?
2. What is the difference between hearing and listening?
3. Is there a non-verbal component to listening?

ACTIVITY

Part 1: Perceiving Others

1. Organize the class into pairs. Ask each pair to discuss a serious problem you select.
2. After 10 minutes, distribute Perceiving Others activity sheet. Ask each pair to turn back to back and complete the sheet.
3. Tell the students to trade sheets with their partners. Have the students react to their partners' assessment. Ask the students to write their reactions on the activity sheet.

Part 2: Descriptions

1. Explain to the students that sometimes we hear but do not listen. In this exercise, they will investigate what it takes to listen properly.

2. Divide the group into pairs. Ask each person to describe himself to his partner. The description should move from appearance, hobbies, and interests to key values and goals.
3. Ask the students to write down a description of their partners based on the interview.
4. Ask each pair to trade descriptions and respond.
5. Distribute Ten Rules for Perceiving Others activity sheet. Based on what the students have learned from the two activities, have the class draw up general rules that they can use to help them understand others.

DISCUSSION QUESTIONS

1. What effect does voice have on communication?
2. What effect do gestures have on communication?
3. What part of your partner's discussion was most difficult to perceive correctly: physical appearance, body language, or vocal tone?
4. What part of your partner's description was most difficult for you to understand and convey in your summary?

Activity Sheet

Perceiving Others

Instructions: Following your interview, answer the questions below about your partner's non-verbal communication.

APPEARANCE

1. What was my partner's hair color?

2. What was my partner's eye color?

3. What was my partner wearing?

4. Was my partner wearing jewelry?

BODY LANGUAGE

1. What was my partner doing with his hands?

2. How was my partner holding his body?

3. What was my partner's facial expression?

4. How close was my partner sitting?

5. What impression did I get from my partner's body language?

VOICE

1. What was the pitch of my partner's voice? High? Low? Normal?

2. How fast was my partner speaking? Slowly? Quickly? Normally?

3. How loud was my partner speaking?

4. What impression did I get from the way my partner spoke?

Activity Sheet

Ten Rules for Perceiving Others

1.

2.

3.

4.

5.

6.

7.

8.

9.

10.

COMMUNICATE!

Twenty-first century students have many means to contact others. Most rely on modern technology—instant messaging, e-mail—if they can't meet face to face, and few think about which types of communication would be most appropriate or effective for a specific task. In this lesson they will evaluate various types of communication.

OBJECTIVES

Upon completing this lesson, the students will be able to evaluate and choose the type of communication that is most effective in achieving a goal.

MATERIALS NEEDED

Communicate! activity sheet (copy for each student)

TEACHER TIPS

Make sure that in discussing forms of communication, students mention traditional methods of making contact (in person, letter, telephone) as well as 21st century methods (e-mail, chat rooms, Web pages, etc.).
Include in-person communication for each of the exercises.

OPENING QUESTIONS

1. What are some of the ways people establish contact with one another?
2. Do these ways have anything in common?

ACTIVITY

1. Ask the class to list the various means of communication available to them. Remember to include person-to-person meeting.
2. Tell the class that they will be role playing a situation in which one person has to ask another for a favor using various means of communication. Ask them which three or four forms of communication they think would be appropriate for this request.

3. Distribute Communicate! activity sheet and divide the class into pairs. Tell one member of a pair (Mr. Seek) to ask a favor of the other (Ms. Grant), using each of the various types of communication the students have listed. (They will have to create artificial Web pages, etc. if these forms of communication are on the list.)
4. Tell the students to write the form of communication they are using on the activity sheet and answer the questions after they have completed the task using that type.
5. Repeat the exercise telling the students that they are to invite their partners to a party. Have the students reverse roles. The student who played Ms. Grant is now Mr. Seek, who is issuing the invitation.
6. Reassemble the class and ask the pairs to report their finding. What parts of the contact were effective? What hindered Mr. Seek from achieving his goal?
7. Lead a discussion on the benefits and drawbacks of various forms of communication and on what skills are needed for effective contact.

DISCUSSION QUESTIONS

1. Are certain forms of communication better than others in certain situations?
2. What are the best ways to establish effective contacts with your peers? With your family? At work?
3. What are the skills you need to make effective contact? Are they the same for all situations?

Communicate!

THE FAVOR

Form of communication: ______________________________

Evaluation:

Ms. Grant:

1. What parts of the contact were easy?

2. What parts of the contact were difficult?

Mr. Seek:

1. What parts of the contact were easy?

2. What parts of the contact were difficult?

3. What hindered Mr. Seek from achieving his goal?

4. How effective was this form of communication in achieving your goal?

THE PARTY

Form of communication: ____

Evaluation:

Mr. Seek (issuing invitation):

1. What parts of the contact were easy?

2. What parts of the contact were difficult?

Ms. Grant (considering the invitation):

1. What parts of the contact were easy?

2. What parts of the contact were difficult?

3. What hindered Mr. Seek from achieving his goal?

4. How effective was this form of communication in achieving your goal?

GET IN CONTACT!

Today's teenagers have become increasingly isolated. They spend their time watching TV and playing videogames, and their personal contacts may be through Internet chat rooms. They often lack such basic person-to-person skills as how to act when meeting someone for the first time. They may be afraid to approach potential social or business contacts or feel awkward when they meet someone new. In this lesson, the students will explore their fears and learn how to make contact with people in a wide variety of situations.

OBJECTIVES

Upon completing this lesson, the students will be able to do the following:

1. Explore the fears they have when meeting people
2. Practice meeting a variety of people in various situations

MATERIALS NEEDED

Making Contact activity sheet (copy for each student)

OPENING QUESTIONS

1. Why do you think people often feel awkward when meeting someone for the first time?
2. Why are first contacts important?

ACTIVITY

1. Distribute Making Contact activity sheet and review. Ask the students to complete the sheet.
2. Have the class share the situations that make them nervous.
3. Ask the students to create a master list of some of the types of contacts they might face. These could include contacts with older people; contacts with other teens; permanent business contacts, such as meeting a boss for the first time; temporary functional contacts, such as meeting a computer repair person; and episodic contacts, such as meeting another resident of their apartment house. Write the list on the board.
4. Divide the class into small groups and tell them to brainstorm how they would act when meeting a person in each contact situation on the master list. Also ask them to suggest what not to do in each situation.

5. Reassemble the class and have the students draw up a master guide called "How to Act on First Contact." Suggest the guide have two sections: the first giving approximately 10 general guidelines on how to act on first meeting someone, and the second suggesting how to act in specific situations.

DISCUSSION QUESTIONS

1. What do we need to do to make meeting people enjoyable?
2. What do we have to do to make the contact beneficial?

Making Contact

Instructions: Complete the following questionnaire listing the situations in which you feel uncomfortable and those in which you feel happy when meeting people for the first time.

A: I'M UNCOMFORTABLE

I feel uncomfortable when I meet the following types of people for the first time:

1.

2.

3.

4.

5.

I feel uncomfortable when I meet people for the first time under the following circumstances:

1.

2.

3.

4.

5.

I feel uncomfortable when I meet people for the first time in the following places:

1.

2.

3.

4.

5.

I feel uncomfortable meeting people when they act like the following:

1.

2.

3.

4.

5.

B. I FEEL HAPPY WHEN I MEET PEOPLE WHO

1.

2.

3.

4.

5.

NEGOTIATING

Negotiations do not take place just between countries or between large organizations. We negotiate all the time—with our family, our friends, and our colleagues. Often, young people believe that negotiation must be confrontational, a situation in which they must win and the other person lose. However, tolerance requires that we approach negotiations with a goal of finding a mutually agreeable solution to a problem. This is win-win negotiation. In this lesson students formally negotiate a theoretical problem, but they can use the skills they learn here in informal settings.

OBJECTIVES

Upon completing this lesson, students will understand the following:

1. The importance of win-win negotiation
2. The steps involved in negotiation

MATERIALS NEEDED

The Basic Rules of Win-Win Negotiating resource sheet (copy for each student)
Five Steps in Negotiating resource sheet (copy for each student)

TEACHER TIPS

Make sure you remain independent when observing the student negotiations.

OPENING QUESTIONS

1. What does it mean to "play hardball"?
2. How have you or your parents felt when negotiating to buy a house or car?
3. How do you feel when you lose an argument?

ACTIVITY

1. Write "win-lose" and "win-win" on the board and define the terms.

2. Divide the class into pairs. Present a local issue important to the class (such as a school problem) and assign positions on the problem. Have each pair negotiate the issue from its position using the win-lose strategy. Give the class members time to prepare their positions as well as to carry out the negotiation. After a few minutes, ask the students how their negotiations are progressing. How do they feel about the negotiations?
3. Tell the class that in a tolerant society we should use a win-win strategy whenever possible. Distribute The Basic Rules of Win-Win Negotiating and Five Steps in Negotiating and review.
4. Ask the pairs to reassemble and negotiate using a win-win strategy. Give the class time to prepare their positions as well as to carry out the negotiation.
5. Reassemble the class and ask the students how their negotiations went. How did they feel about the negotiations this time?

DISCUSSION QUESTIONS

1. Are there any circumstances under which win-lose negotiation would be appropriate?
2. What are the long-term benefits of win-win negotiation?
3. Are there drawbacks to win-win negotiation?

Resource Sheet

The Basic Rules of Win-Win Negotiating

- **Each party has equal rights and deserves equal respect.**
- **Negotiations should take place in comfortable conditions in a neutral setting.**
- **Parties should be positive when entering the negotiation.**
- **Parties should keep their emotions under control.**
- **Parties should separate the people from the problem.**
- **Parties should approach the issue as a problem they can solve.**
- **Parties must express their positions clearly and concisely.**
- **Parties should base their arguments on objective criteria, not emotions.**
- **Each party must listen attentively to the arguments of the other and carefully explore them.**
- **Parties should think creatively, seeking a mutually acceptable compromise.**
- **Parties must respect and abide by the outcome of the negotiation.**

Resource Sheet

Five Steps in Negotiating

1. **Define the Problem**

   Clearly articulate the problem.

   Research the specific issues involved in the problem.

2. **Define Goals**

   What do you want to get out of the negotiation?

   What do you expect the other person wants?

3. **Define Positions**

   What are you willing to give the other person?

   What does the other person have that you might want?

4. **Work toward a Mutual Goal**

   Explore your position and that of the other person to find a mutually agreeable solution that gives you both as much of what you want as possible.

   Generate a variety of options.

5. **Find a Solution**

   Ideally, you will find that the other person wants what you are willing to give and you are prepared to give what the other person wants.

CHAPTER 6
CREATIVE THINKING AND DECISION MAKING

This chapter teaches students two important skills that they can apply to many situations throughout their lives: creative thinking and decision making. The first four sessions introduce various methods of creative thinking and problem solving. The fifth lesson emphasizes decision making as a clearly articulated process. The final lesson discusses the types of decision making students will encounter in their lives.

SESSIONS

CREATIVE THINKING

Brainstorming

Free Association

Sleep on It!

Tree Diagrams

DECISION MAKING

Steps in Decision Making

Types of Decision Making

BRAINSTORMING

Brainstorming is one of the most effective ways of generating a large number of original ideas and determining how best to solve a problem. In this session students brainstorm how to use a grant for their school.

OBJECTIVES

Upon completing this lesson, the students will understand the process of brainstorming.

MATERIALS NEEDED

The Brainstorming Process resource sheet (copy for each student)
Brainstorming activity sheet (copy for each student)

TEACHER TIPS

Brainstorming works best in groups of eight to ten. Small groups will not generate enough ideas; in larger groups, everyone may not have an opportunity to participate.

OPENING QUESTION

How do people come up with ideas?

ACTIVITY

1. Tell the students that a noted philanthropist has given their school $1 million, and their class has been asked to decide how to spend it. Tell the class that they will use brainstorming to come to their decision. Distribute The Brainstorming Process resource sheet and discuss.
2. Divide the class into groups of eight to ten students. Distribute Brainstorming activity sheet and review. Tell the groups to begin their session.
3. Once the groups have determined the best use of the money, reassemble the class and have the groups share their results. Ask the students to reflect on their brainstorming experience.

DISCUSSION QUESTIONS

1. What are the benefits of brainstorming?
2. What are the drawbacks?
3. Why is it important not to criticize people's ideas when brainstorming?

Resource Sheet

The Brainstorming Process

Step 1: Define the Problem

Write a concise definition of the problem that everyone can agree on.

Step 2: Give Yourself a Time Limit

Determine how much time you want to devote to brainstorming. Twenty-five minutes is a good period.

Step 3: Generate Ideas

Shout out as many ideas as possible and record them. Do not criticize the ideas or even think about them. Make sure that everyone has a chance to participate.

Step 4: Pare Down Ideas

Select the five ideas the group likes best.

Step 5: Develop Criteria

Develop the criteria you will use to evaluate the ideas. Start the criteria with "it should . . ."

Step 6: Evaluating Ideas

Use a numerical scoring system to evaluate each idea based on the criteria.

Step 7: Announce the Winning Idea

The idea with the highest score will be the winner.

Brainstorming

Instructions: A noted philanthropist is donating $1 million to your school. Your group is to decide how it should be spent. Use brainstorming to find the best idea.

Ideas:

Five Ideas We Like Best:

1.

2.

3.

4.

5.

Criteria We Will Use to Judge the Ideas:

1. It should:

2. It should:

3. It should:

4. It should:

5. It should:

Analyzing Our Choices

Idea	Criteria					Total Ranking
1.	1.	2.	3.	4.	5.	
2.						
3.						
4.						
5.						

Give each idea a score of 0 (awful) to 5 (great!), depending on how well it meets each criterion. Add up the scores to find the total ranking. The idea with the highest score is the one you should use.

Our Best Idea:

FREE ASSOCIATION

Free association can often result in creative solutions to problems because it reduces the barrier between the conscious and subconscious. Students rarely know about this technique, and those that have heard of it often mistrust it because it does not seem logical. This lesson should make them more comfortable with the process.

OBJECTIVES

Upon completing this lesson, the students will understand how to use free association to solve a problem.

MATERIALS NEEDED

Free Association resource sheet (copy for each student)

TEACHER TIPS

Students are often reluctant to express free associations because they fear criticism. Remind them that only they will know what they have written.

This approach works best for individuals, but small groups can use it as well.

OPENING QUESTIONS

1. With what smell do you associate joy?
2. With what animal or other element of nature would you associate yourself?

ACTIVITY

1. Ask the participants to sit in a circle. Say a word and ask the student on your right to say the first thing he thinks of when he hears your word. Repeat the process until all students have contributed a word.
2. Explain that students can use this type of free association to develop ideas and solve problems.
3. Distribute Free Association resource sheet and review.

4. Give the students a problem, perhaps one that involves their school or their local community, and run through the steps on the sheet using the problem.
5. Explain that this type of problem solving works best when used by an individual rather than a group. Ask each student to think of her own problem and repeat the exercise.

DISCUSSION QUESTIONS

1. Why do you think this type of problem solving works best when used by an individual rather than a group?
2. What are the benefits of using this method?
3. What are the drawbacks?
4. What was your reaction to this type of problem solving?

Resource Sheet

Free Association

Step 1: Define the Problem

Write down your problem. Choose one or two words that express the essence of your problem. Your association does not have to be logical. Write down these words.

Step 2: Concentrate on the Chosen Words

Relax and empty your mind. Think only of the two words you have chosen to express your problem. As you think of those words, note any other words that come to mind. Don't limit yourself to words you think logical. Write down all words.

Step 3: Concentrate on the Words in Step 2

Chose five or six words your mind generated in Step 2. As you think of those words, note any other words that come to mind. Don't limit yourself to words you think logical. Write down all words.

Step 4: Note Ideas and Thoughts That Start Coming to Mind

Take a big sheet of paper and write whatever thoughts and ideas come to mind from your free associations to this point. Don't edit your thoughts as you write. Note everything, even if it appears illogical or unconnected.

Step 5: Repeat Steps 3 and 4

Repeat Step 3 using five or six of the remaining words you generated in Step 2. Then, note the thoughts and ideas that come from free association with those words.

Step 6: Review Your Notes

If you haven't yet come up with an idea or solution, review your notes. They will suggest new thoughts and associations. The main thing is not to restrict your mind.

Stage 7: Revisit Your Notes the Following Day

The next day, review your notes with a fresh eye.

SLEEP ON IT!

We can often find solutions to problems by gathering information about them and then leaving them alone for a few days. The information seems to miraculously organize itself, and a solution appears. Our subconscious has been at work while our mind has been elsewhere. Students are frequently reluctant to use this type of problem solving, believing that they must focus on an issue until they come to a solution. This lesson shows them how they can solve a problem—if they just sleep on it!

OBJECTIVES

Upon completing this lesson, the students will understand how they can solve a problem by stepping away from it.

MATERIALS NEEDED

Sleep on It resource sheet (copy for each student)

TEACHER TIPS

Students may be reluctant to suggest answers or may want to think before they respond. Remind everyone to be non-judgmental about the responses. The point is not to think about the answers—just say the first thing that comes to mind.

OPENING QUESTION

What do we mean when we say, "I'll sleep on it"?

ACTIVITY

1. Suggest a problem and provide the class with some background information.
2. Ask the students to organize the background information.
3. Ask the students to immediately suggest three possible solutions to the problem and write them on a sheet of paper. They should write the first thoughts that come to mind.
4. Ask the students to evaluate the solutions based on the background you have given them, and choose the best solution.

5. Explain that our subconscious operates in the same way as the students did in the exercise. It organizes information and analyzes solutions while our minds work on other things.
6. Distribute Sleep on It resource sheet and review.
7. Ask the class to solve a problem—it may be one in their school or community—using the Sleep on It technique. Give them one week to research it and come up with a solution.

DISCUSSION QUESTIONS

1. What are the benefits of using this method?
2. What are the drawbacks?
3. What was your reaction to this type of problem solving?

Sleep on It

Step 1: Load the Problem

Formulate the problem in as much detail as possible. By defining the problem, you are also "loading" it into your subconscious. When you are more experienced with this technique, you can also "load" the amount of time you need to find an answer.

Step 2: Accumulate Information

Accumulate as much information as you can about the problem. Do not try to direct your research or to filter the information you find. Do not try to organize your data.

Step 3: Incubate

Set the problem aside so that your subconscious can work on it.

Step 4: Forget It

Do something else. Don't think about the problem. Albert Einstein used to play the violin to take his mind off a problem he could not solve. You can sleep, play sports, enjoy a hobby—whatever will distract your mind. Do not try to rush a solution, and don't be afraid that you will not find a solution. Trust your mind!

Step 5: Trigger It

At some point your subconscious will solve the problem and "deliver" the answer to your conscious mind. Any word, movement—anything at all—can bring the answer to light.

TREE DIAGRAMS

One of the most effective ways of analyzing problems, objectives, or decisions is to create a tree diagram. Information is organized on a tree-like chart, with the trunk representing the main problem or issue, the branches representing outcomes, and the roots signifying the causes or influences. These trees can help students understand the underlying causes of a problem and analyze their objectives or the impact of their solutions.

OBJECTIVES

Upon completing this lesson, the students will understand how to use tree diagrams to analyze a problem.

MATERIALS NEEDED

Activity 1: Decision Tree (copy for each student)
Activity 2: Problem–Cause resource sheet (copy for each student)
Problem–Cause Diagram (copy for each student)
Index cards
Tape

OPENING QUESTIONS

1. How do you plot strategy in chess?
2. How can creating a visual representation of a problem help you solve it?

ACTIVITIES

ACTIVITY 1: DECISION TREE

1. Tell the class that one of the most effective tools they can use to analyze problems and determine objectives is the tree diagram. The main issue is represented by the tree's trunk, and the relevant factors, influences, and outcomes show up as systems of roots and branches.
2. Explain that one of the simplest uses of a tree diagram is to determine the costs and benefits of a particular action. This type of diagram is called a decision tree. In its simplest form a person writes down a decision and then determines two effects of that decision. She then determines two effects of each of the initial two decisions.

3. Distribute Decision Tree and ask the students to determine, using a decision tree, whether it is better to bag their groceries in paper or in plastic.

ACTIVITY 2: PROBLEM–CAUSE DIAGRAM

1. Explain that tree diagrams can also be used to show the causes and effects of a problem and how various issues are linked. These diagrams are called problem–cause trees. Distribute Problem–Cause resource sheet and Problem–Cause Diagram and discuss.
2. Ask the students to create a problem–cause tree using a problem they have in school, for example, poor conditions in the cafeteria. Write the core problem in the middle of the board.
3. Distribute index cards to the students and ask them to write a negative statement describing the situation they are analyzing.
4. Post the cards where everyone can see them. Tell the students that they are now going to determine how their statements are related to the problem—some are causes and some are effects. Ask the students to sort the cards into the two categories. Place the causes below the problem and the effects above them. Place those statements over which the students have no control to the side. Clarify or discard any statements that are unclear.
5. Ask the students to arrange the causes so that the class can see how they are related to each other. The goal is to create a roadmap showing how one problem leads to another, and how these problems are related to the core problem. They should arrange the causes below the problem on the board. Review the causes and ask if any important causes are missing.
6. Follow the same procedure for the effects, but have them arrange the effects above the problem on the board.
7. Check the logic of the tree and tell the students to copy the tree onto a piece of paper.

ACTIVITY 3: SOLUTION TREE

1. Tell the students that a third type of tree diagram is an objective or solution tree. They can create a solution tree from their problem–cause tree by rephrasing their negative statements (problems) as positive outcomes.
2. Ask the students to create a solution tree for the core problem they have been analyzing.

DISCUSSION QUESTIONS

1. What are the benefits of using tree diagrams in decision making and problem analysis?
2. What are the drawbacks?

DECISION TREE

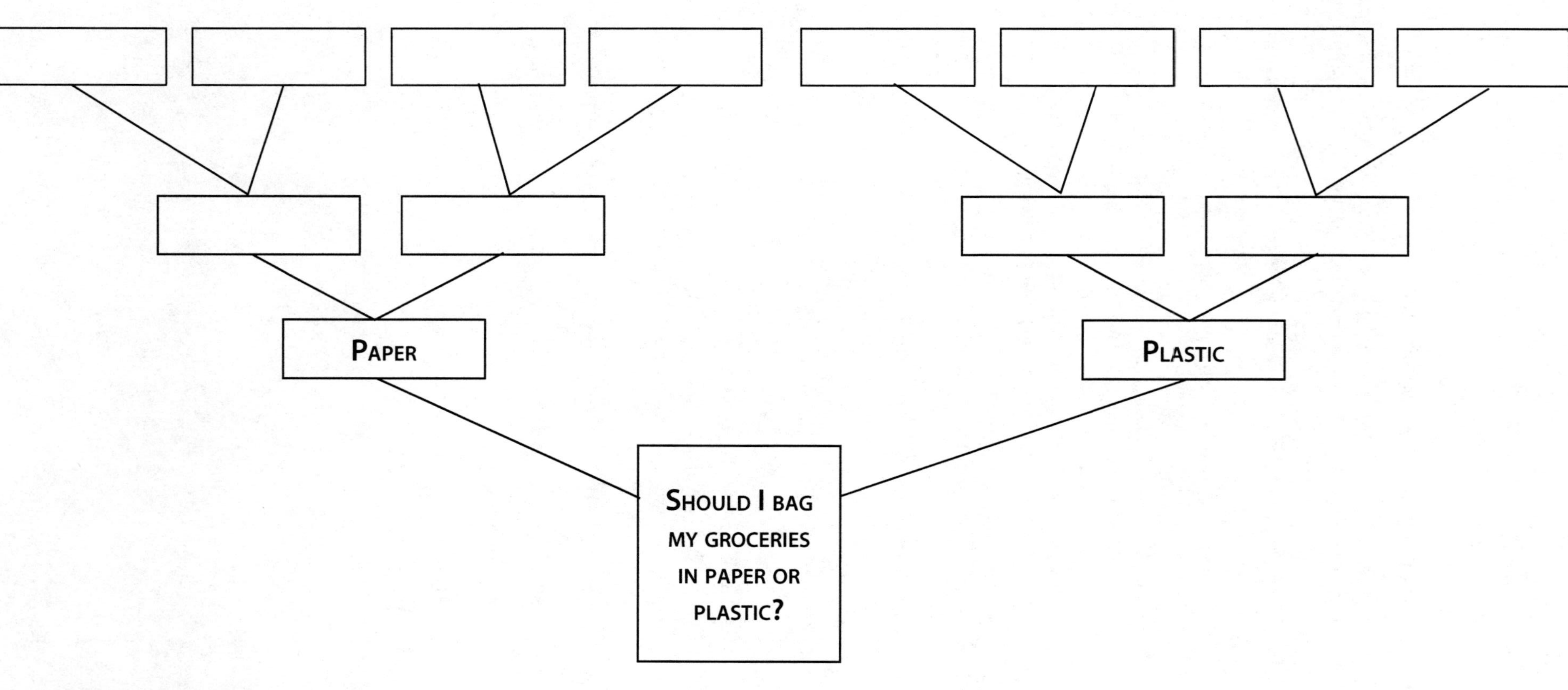

Problem–Cause Tree

Step 1: Determine the Problem

Write a concise definition of the problem that everyone can agree on in the center of a chalk- or clipboard.

Step 2: Develop Negative Statements about the Problem

List negative statements describing the situation they are analyzing. Write these on index cards and post the cards where everyone can see them.

Step 3: Examine the Negative Statements

Examine the negative statements, determining how they are related to the core problem. Are they causes or effects? Place the causes below the problem and the effects above.

Step 4: Analyze Causes

Arrange the causes, indicating their relationship to one another. The goal is to create a simple diagram showing how one problem leads to another and how these problems are related to the core problem. Add any important causes you think are missing.

Step 5: Analyze Effects

Repeat Step 4 for effects.

Step 6: Check Your Logic

Check the logic of the tree and copy it to a sheet of paper, using lines and arrows to show the links between the various elements.

Problem–Cause Diagram

Below is a sample tree diagram illustrating some of the causes and effects of deforestation.

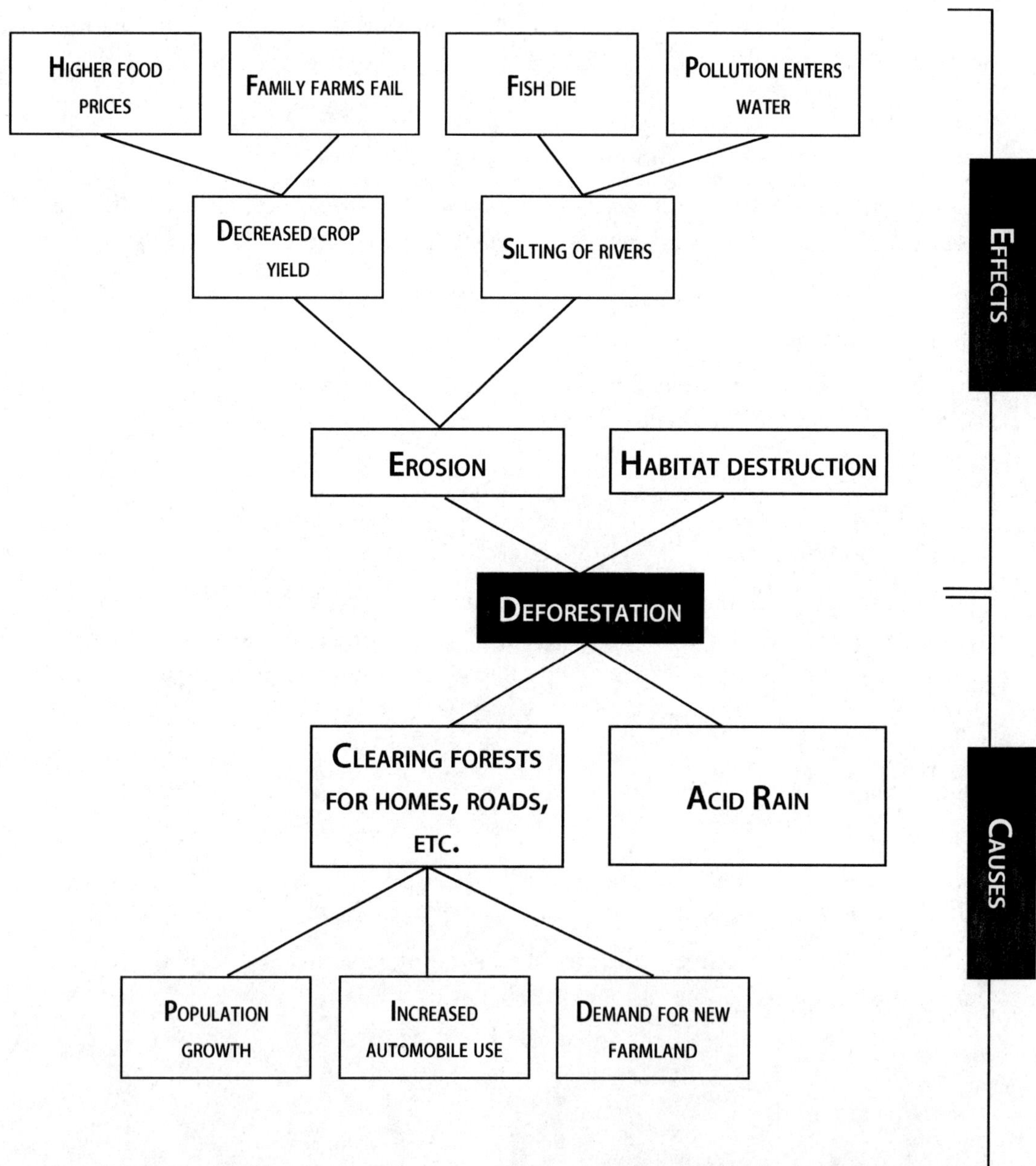

STEPS IN DECISION MAKING

Teenagers often make decisions based on emotion or gut reaction. This lesson teaches them that decision making is a process they can use in a variety of situations.

OBJECTIVES

Upon completing this lesson, the students will understand the seven steps in decision making.

MATERIALS NEEDED

Seven Steps in Decision Making resource sheet (copy for each student)

OPENING QUESTIONS

1. What do we mean when we say: "If a person makes a decision she controls the situation; if she doesn't the situation controls her"?
2. How do you usually make decisions?

ACTIVITY

Part 1: Seven Steps

1. Distribute Seven Steps in Decision Making resource sheet and review.
2. Ask the students to use the decision-making model to make a simple decision in their daily life, for example, what to wear or whether to go to a movie.

Part 2: Decision Making Across the Board

1. Explain that the seven-step model of decision making can be used in organization settings as well as in personal situations.
2. Divide the class into four groups: family, non-profit organization, business, and government.
3. Ask each group to develop a situation in which the group must make a decision.
4. Tell the groups to use the seven steps to make the decision for their organizations.
5. Reassemble the class and have each group describe how it applied the model.

DISCUSSION QUESTIONS

1. What was the most difficult step in the process? Why?
2. Why is it important to review and evaluate the decision?
3. What are the pluses and minuses of this process?

Resource Sheet

Seven Steps in Decision Making

1. IDENTIFY THE DECISION TO BE MADE

2. GATHER THE INFORMATION NEEDED TO MAKE THE DECISION

3. IDENTIFY THE ALTERNATIVES

4. ESTABLISH THE CRITERIA FOR MAKING THE DECISION

5. CHOOSE AMONG THE ALTERNATIVES

6. TAKE ACTION

7. REVIEW AND EVALUATE THE DECISION

TYPES OF DECISION MAKING

This lesson familiarizes students with the types of decision making used in various organizations. These methods can range from decision by majority vote in legislatures and by committee vote in co-op boards to decision by an individual in the military and in some business situations. Students learn about the various types of decision making they may encounter, and discuss the benefits and problems of each.

OBJECTIVES

Upon completing this lesson, the students will understand the following:

1. That there are many ways to make decisions
2. The benefits and drawbacks of each method

MATERIALS NEEDED

Methods of Decision Making activity sheet (copy for each student)

TEACHER TIPS

Remind the students to think about various types of organizations—business, social, political, military, etc.—as they evaluate the various types of decision making.

OPENING QUESTIONS

1. Are all decisions made in the same way?
2. What kinds of decision-making methods do we see in our daily lives?

ACTIVITY

1. Explain to the students that although in the last session they learned about the decision-making process, they will encounter different types of decision making throughout their lives. This lesson will famliarize them with the most significant types and help the students evaluate each.

2. Write the five main types of decision making on the board:
   - by majority vote
   - by experts
   - by small group
   - by consensus
   - by one individual
3. Divide the class into five groups and distribute the activity sheets.
4. Assign each group a type of decision making and ask the groups to brainstorm the advantages and disadvantages of the type as well as the situations in which their type might be beneficial or harmful. Tell them to note their findings on their activity sheets.
5. Reassemble the class and ask each team to report its findings. Ask the class to add anything they think important to the team reports.
6. Write the team findings on the board and have the students create a master list of decision-making types.

DISCUSSION QUESTIONS

1. Are some methods of making decisions always better than others?
2. Are some methods appropriate for some kinds of organizations but not for others?
3. What would happen if a society adopted only one type of decision making?

Activity Sheet

Methods of Decision Making

Instructions:

1. Write the method of decision making you are assigned at the top of the chart.
2. Brainstorm the advantages and disadvantages of the method and think of the situations in which the method would be beneficial or harmful.

Method of Decision Making: ______________________________

Advantages	Disadvantages	Will Work in the Following Situations	Will Not Work in the Following Situations
1.			
2.			
3.			
4.			
5.			

PART III
Contribution

CHAPTER 7
PARTICIPATION AND COLLABORATION

In this chapter students examine the importance of an active life in achieving their personal goals and in bettering their society and they learn how to participate in an atmosphere of tolerance. The first three lessons discuss the students' responsibilities to society. They discover that with rights come responsibilities and that they must work together if they are to better themselves and solve the problems of their community, nation, and world. The last four lessons teach students how to work together as teams.

SESSIONS

Participating
Rights and Responsibilities
Individual and Society
Teams
Leadership Qualities
Leadership Styles
The Leader and the Team

PARTICIPATING

In this lesson students learn the importance of being an active participant in life. They will discover the difference between a passive life style, one in which an individual is an observer of society, and a life of active involvement, one in which an individual contributes to the betterment of society. They will discover that they can only reach their potential by becoming actively involved with others. They will also realize the importance of active involvement in solving the problems of their world.

OBJECTIVES

Upon competing this lesson, students will understand the following:

1. The meaning of activism
2. The meaning of an active involvement

MATERIALS NEEDED

Your Task activity sheet (copy for each student)
Two Approaches activity sheet (copy for each student)

OPENING QUESTION

What does the saying "An active person proposes and makes; the passive one begs and waits" mean?

ACTIVITY

Part 1: Active vs. Passive

1. Distribute Your Task activity sheet, placing it face down on each student's desk. Tell the students that they are not to turn the paper over until your signal, at which point they are to complete the tasks outlined as quickly as possible.
2. Give the signal and have the class complete the tasks.
3. Once everyone has finished, ask the students if what they did was an example of activism. What elements are needed to turn "activity" into "activism"?
4. Distribute Two Approaches activity sheet. Tell the class that there are two ways to approach life: actively and passively. Write the two terms on the board and have the class brainstorm what each approach involves. Tell the students to write their thoughts on their activity sheets.

5. Ask the students if it is possible to achieve their potential if they view life passively.
6. Ask the students to write down three qualities they possess that are important in cultivating an active involvement in life.
7. Have the class share answers and develop a master list of what is involved in an active outlook on life and the qualities needed to pursue it.

Part 2: What I Can Do

1. Tell the students that they are now going to put their active outlook into practice. Ask them to list what they could do for

    a. their friends

    b. their class

    c. their family

    that would benefit both parties and make life interesting for all involved.
2. Ask them to write down one problem they would like to address in their lives.

DISCUSSION QUESTIONS

1. Why is active involvement in life important to the development of a tolerant society?
2. How can a passive attitude toward life result in intolerance?

Activity Sheet

Your Task

1. Stand up as fast as possible
2. Shout aloud, "I will do this faster than anybody!!!"
3. Read this list attentively
4. Jump 10 times on your right leg
5. Run from one wall to the other one and touch each
6. Laugh loudly at the instructor
7. Shout your name twice
8. Imitate your favorite animal
9. Come back quickly to your place
10. After you have finished reading the text attentively, do only points 11 and 12
11. Sit down on the floor
12. Put the task paper in front of you

Activity Sheet

Two Approaches

Passive Life Style	Active Life Style
1.	1.
2.	2.
3.	3.
4.	4.
5.	5.

Three Qualities Important to My Active Life Style

1.

2.

3.

What I Can Do for My:

A. Friends

B. Class

C. Family

One Problem I Would Like to Address in My Life:

RIGHTS AND RESPONSIBILITIES

Contemporary students often focus on their rights but ignore the fact that with rights come responsibilities. This lesson asks them to review the rights they have in their family, school, society, and nation and then think carefully about the responsibilities these rights entail.

OBJECTIVES

Upon completing this lesson, students will be able to do the following:

1. Understand that rights also involve responsibilities
2. Articulate key rights and responsibilities

MATERIALS NEEDED

Rights and Responsibilities activity sheet (copy for each student)

OPENING QUESTIONS

1. Define *rights*.
2. Can you have rights without responsibilities toward others?
3. What would happen if people were not obliged to do anything for others?

ACTIVITY

1. Distribute Rights and Responsibilities activity sheet. Ask the students to think of rights they have as members of their family. Tell them to write these in the appropriate space on the activity sheet. Then ask them to think of the responsibilities that result from each right and write these on the activity sheet.
2. Ask the students to think of rights they have as members of their school. Tell them to write these in the appropriate space on the activity sheet. Then ask them to think of the responsibilities that result from each right and write these on the activity sheet.
3. Ask the students to think of rights they have as members of their society. Tell them to write these in the appropriate space on the activity sheet. Then ask them to think of the responsibilities that result from each right and write these on the activity sheet.
4. Ask the students to think of rights they have as members of their country. Tell them to write these in the appropriate space on the activity sheet. Then ask them to think of the responsibilities that result from each right and write these on the activity sheet.

5. Once the students have completed their activity sheets, ask them to discuss their findings and create a master list.

DISCUSSION QUESTIONS

1. Can we build a tolerant society based only on rights?
2. Do we have the same rights and responsibilities in all areas (family, school, etc.) of our life?

Activity Sheet

Rights and Responsibilities

Instructions: Think of rights you have as a member of your family, school, society, and nation. Think of the responsibilities associated with these rights.

FAMILY

Rights	Responsibilities
1.	1.
2.	2.
3.	3.
4.	4.
5.	5.

SCHOOL

Rights	Responsibilities
1.	1.
2.	2.
3.	3.
4.	4.
5.	5.

SOCIETY

Rights	Responsibilities
1.	1.
2.	2.
3.	3.
4.	4.
5.	5.

NATION

Rights	Responsibilities
1.	1.
2.	2.
3.	3.
4.	4.
5.	5.

INDIVIDUAL AND SOCIETY

By the time we are adults, we have learned that we cannot "go it alone." We must work with other people in organizations or in the larger society to achieve our individual goals and the goals that we have for our community, nation, and world. We have also learned that by working together we actually expand our possibilities. This lesson encourages students to work toward this understanding.

OBJECTIVES

In this session students will learn the following:

1. The importance of working together to achieve personal and societal goals
2. The importance of society in their lives

MATERIALS NEEDED

Individual and Society activity sheet (copy for each student)
Pictures or photos for each group cut into small pieces and assembled into packets, one for each group (the pictures should be complicated so that the students will be challenged to reassemble them)

OPENING QUESTIONS

1. What does "one man, no man" mean?
2. What does society contribute to the individual?
3. What does the individual contribute to society?

ACTIVITY

1. Organize the class into groups. Remove one piece from each packet of picture pieces and distribute the packets to each group.
2. Tell the groups to reassemble the pictures. The winner is the first group to discover that one fragment is missing.
3. Ask the students to evaluate their experience of working with groups. How was working with others helpful? How did it slow the activity down?
4. Distribute Individual and Society activity sheet. Ask the students to list what people can do by themselves, without friends or support from other people.

5. Now ask them to list what they can accomplish by collaborating with others and using all the support mechanisms society offers. Have the students share their lists.
6. Ask the students to list 10 things that society gives them. Discuss their suggestions and create a master list.

DISCUSSION QUESTIONS

1. How important is society in achieving your goals?
2. In what ways is society important?
3. Can society hinder achievement?

Activity Sheet

Individual and Society

Part 1: Me and Others

Instructions:

1. In the first column, list all the things you can do by yourself, without help from anyone else.
2. In the second column, list the things you can do with the help of friends, your community, and society in general.

What I Can Do by Myself	What I Can Do with the Help of Friends and Society

Part 2: Society and Me

Instructions: List 10 things society gives you.

10 THINGS SOCIETY GIVES ME:

1.

2.

3.

4.

5.

6.

7.

8.

9.

10.

TEAMS

Working within a group encourages tolerance. To make the group successful, participants must understand the factors that can contribute to or hinder group cohesion and prevent the group from doing its job. They must be willing to negotiate and compromise, and think creatively about solutions that might be acceptable to the entire group. This activity helps students understand how groups work and helps them develop the skills they need to work with others.

OBJECTIVES

Upon completing this lesson, students will understand the following:

1. The factors important in making a group successful
2. The roles they must play if the group is to succeed

MATERIALS NEEDED

none

TEACHER TIPS

Make sure that the groups do not become hostile to the "buyers" and that they are willing to negotiate the sale.

OPENING QUESTIONS

1. Why do some organizations succeed while others fail?
2. What does "group cohesion" mean?
3. Must a group be cohesive to succeed?

ACTIVITY

Part 1: A Sale

1. Divide the class into small groups of six or seven. Ask one student to step out of each group. You can select that student by counting off. (Give each person a number and have all number threes, for example, step out of their groups.) These are the "buyers." The students remaining in the groups are the "sellers."

2. Tell the buyers that they must negotiate the purchase of a small commercial building. They can work together with other buyers to negotiate the sale with one group of sellers, or they can try to negotiate individually.
3. Remind the sellers that they must negotiate; they cannot refuse to sell. Give the students 15 minutes to complete the activity.

Part 2: Evaluating Teamwork

1. Reassemble the class and discuss what the students learned about teamwork from the activity.
2. Ask the students to suggest factors that help consolidate a group and make it work efficiently. Factors they suggest might be these:
    - Trust
    - Mutual respect
    - Common goals
    - Willingness of members to compromise
    - Positive atmosphere
    - Willingness to share tasks
    - Willingness to make use of the unique skills and qualities of each participant
    - Creative thinking
3. Now ask the students to suggest factors that might prevent a group from consolidating and working efficiently. Factors they suggest might be these:
    - Uncertainty of purpose
    - Intolerant attitudes
    - Manipulative behavior
    - Pressures from one member on another
    - Failure of members to act in a responsible manner
    - Failure to acknowledge the unique skills and contributions of participants
    - Hostile atmosphere

DISCUSSION QUESTIONS

1. Do you think it is easier to work as in individual or with a group?
2. What was is easiest part of working with a group? The hardest?

LEADERSHIP QUALITIES

Teenagers frequently do not want to become leaders or think they do not have leadership qualities. Often they equate "leader" with politics. In this session, the students learn that there are leaders in every field and that while some leadership qualities may be unique to specific fields, there are traits that most leaders have in common. Finally, they begin to understand that everyone possesses leadership qualities and that they have qualities they may never thought they had.

OBJECTIVES

Upon completing this lesson, students will be able to identify the following:

1. The qualities important in leaders
2. The leadership qualities they possess

MATERIALS NEEDED

Leadership Qualities activity sheet (copy for each student)

TEACHER TIPS

Make sure that the class compiles a diverse list of men and women from a variety of fields—science, the arts, education, business, etc.

OPENING QUESTIONS

1. Why are some people leaders and others not?
2. Can everyone be a leader?

ACTIVITY

1. Ask the class to compile a list of leaders they have studied in history class. Write the names on the board. Ask the class to name contemporary individuals they consider leaders. Write the names on the board.
2. Divide the class into small groups. Assign or ask each group to choose a name from the history column and from the contemporary column. Ask each group to brainstorm the qualities that made their individuals leaders.

3. Have each group report their findings to the entire class. Compile a master list of leadership characteristics. Some of the qualities they may suggest are these:
    - Determination
    - Daring
    - Vision
    - Ambition
    - Moral courage
    - Charisma
    - Ability to communicate
    - Intuition
4. Ask the class if any of the leadership qualities they have suggested are situational. Are there qualities that leaders in one field must have that leaders in another don't have to have?
5. Distribute Leadership Qualities activity sheet. Ask the class to determine which qualities all leaders *must* have in order to succeed. Tell them to enter these qualities on their activity sheets.
6. Now ask them to check off the qualities they think they already have.
7. Ask the students to list the leadership qualities they possess that will be important in the career field they are investigating.
8. Explain that they may never have thought of themselves as leaders but they may face situations in which they will have to take a leadership role, and they should be prepared for this.

DISCUSSION QUESTIONS

1. Can you acquire leadership qualities or are leaders born? Provide examples to justify your response.
2. Do successful leaders always work for good? Is there a moral component to leadership?
3. Have the qualities important in leaders changed over time?

Activity Sheet

Leadership Qualities

Instructions:

1. List the qualities all leaders must have in the left-hand column.
2. Check off those qualities you think you possess in the right-hand column.
3. List the situational leadership qualities you possess in your field.

Qualities Leaders Must Have	Those Qualities I Have
1.	
2.	
3.	
4.	
5.	
6.	
7.	
8.	
9.	
10.	

Leadership Qualities I Have in My Chosen Field

1.

2.

3.

4.

5.

LEADERSHIP STYLES

Students often think that all leaders have the same style: they approach their role in the same way. In this session, students will learn about the many ways people lead, and they will evaluate the pros and cons of various styles. They will then investigate how group dynamics and leadership styles interact.

OBJECTIVES

Upon completing this lesson, the students will understand the following:

1. The various styles of leadership
2. How groups relate to leadership styles

MATERIALS NEEDED

Leadership Styles activity sheet (copy for each student)
Team/Leader Relationship Styles activity sheet (copy for each student)

OPENING QUESTION

What makes some leaders better than others?

ACTIVITY

Part 1: Situations

1. Distribute Leadership Styles activity sheet and review.
2. Ask the students to determine in what situations each of the leadership styles might be appropriate. (They may determine that some are never appropriate.)
3. Have the students share their findings with the class.

Part 2: Relationships

1. Distribute Team/Leader Relationship Styles activity sheet. Explain that we can make a matrix illustrating the possible combinations of group and leadership styles. There are nine possible combinations illustrating how leaders interact with groups and nine combinations of how groups interact with leaders.
2. Ask the students to enter the pros and cons of each type on the activity sheet.

3. Once the students have completed the assignment, organize a class discussion based on their thoughts.

DISCUSSION QUESTIONS

1. Do you agree that the leader embodies the organization's interests and goals?
2. What does an organization need from its leader?

Leadership Styles

Leadership Styles

Dominant-repressive

Authoritarian. Takes control of the group and represses other points of view. Works with only those team members that support his position. Pressures individuals and acts to realize his goals no matter what the cost.

Dominant-convincing

Dominating, ambitious. Uses his knowledge and experience to dominate others. Explains and argues for his goals.

Guiding

Visionary. "Idea person." Anxious to lead the group in new directions. Develops common goals and shares ideas for achieving them. Attracts people through ideas.

Business

Organizer. Efficiently organizes work, assigns roles and responsibilities. Assumes a high level of personal responsibility for the group's actions. Subordinates achieving the goal to planning and tactics.

Confidential

Delegates. Selects people with the talents he needs and delegates responsibility to them. Develops general strategy but holds the people he has chosen totally accountable for achieving the group's goals.

Consultative

Works to satisfy the will of the majority. Delegates responsibilities among group members. Shares information, strategies, and goals. Attracts experts and advisers. Commonly reveals optimal methods, tactics, strategies.

Executive

Executes the team's decisions. Is devoted to representing the interests of those who made him their leader. Assumes personal responsibility for results and mistakes.

Shady

Manipulates individuals. Works from a hidden agenda.

Instructions:

Determine the situations in which each leadership style might be appropriate. There might be some styles you think are never appropriate.

LEADERSHIP STYLE	WHEN APPROPRIATE
Dominant–repressive	
Dominant–convincing	
Guiding	
Business	
Confidential	
Consultative	
Executive	
Shady	

Activity Sheet

Team/Leader Relationship Styles

Relationships Styles Team to Leader		Relationship Styles Leader to Team	
Team	**Leader**	**Team**	**Leader**
Demanding	Confrontational	Overbearing	Confrontational
Reasonable	Reasonable	Reasonable	Reasonable
Subordinate	Conciliatory	Compliant	Conciliatory

STYLE: ______________________ X ______________________

Pros: ____

____

____

Cons: ____

____

____

STYLE: ______________________ X ______________________

Pros: ____

____

____

Cons: ____

____

____

STYLE: ______________________________ X ______________________________

Pros: ______________________________

____

____

Cons: ______________________________

____

____

STYLE: ______________________________ X ______________________________

Pros: ______________________________

____

____

Cons: ______________________________

____

____

STYLE: ______________________________ X ______________________________

Pros: ______________________________

____

____

Cons: ______________________________

____

____

STYLE: ______________________________ X ______________________________

Pros: ______________________________

____

____

Cons: ______________________________

____

____

STYLE: ______________________________ **X** ______________________________

Pros: ____

____

____

Cons: ____

____

____

STYLE: ______________________________ **X** ______________________________

Pros: ____

____

____

Cons: ____

____

____

STYLE: ______________________________ **X** ______________________________

Pros: ____

____

____

Cons: ____

____

____

THE LEADER AND THE TEAM

Everyone will probably be a leader at some point, just as everyone will be a member of a team or organization. To function efficiently as a team, each member must understand the concerns and expectations of the others. In this lesson students play the role of team leader so that they can better understand what leaders expect of themselves and of their teams.

OBJECTIVES

Upon completing this lesson, the students will understand the relationship between the leader and the team.

MATERIALS NEEDED

The Leader and the Team activity sheet (copy for each student)

OPENING QUESTIONS

1. What does it mean to "put yourself in someone else's shoes"?
2. Why is mutual understanding important in organizations?

ACTIVITY

1. Tell the students that they are going to put themselves in someone else's shoes: those of a new team leader. Ask them how they would feel if they were suddenly put in charge of a group that had to accomplish an important task.
2. Distribute The Leader and the Team activity sheet and review. Ask the students to imagine that they have been chosen to lead a new team that has to accomplish an important task. Tell them that they can decide what kind of team this will be and the task it must accomplish. Ask them to describe their team and its task in Part 1 of the activity sheet.
3. Explain that good leaders can clearly articulate the expectations they have for themselves and for the members of their team. Ask the students to answer the questions in Part 2 of the activity sheet as clearly as possible. Remind them that while many of their answers may be situational, dependent on the team and its specific goal, leaders often have requirements that are common to all situations. They are to emphasize these common requirements in their answers.
4. Have the students share their answers. Develop a master list of the common requirements for each question.

DISCUSSION QUESTIONS

1. How can understanding the concerns of leaders make a team successful?
2. Why must leaders understand the concerns of their teams?

Activity Sheet

The Leader and the Team

Instructions: Assume that you are the new leader of a team that you have just formed. You can determine what type of team (business, social, political, etc.) this is and what its goal will be. Describe your goal and your team and then answer the questions about your leadership.

Part 1:

MY TEAM:

MY GOAL:

Part 2:

MY LEADERSHIP:

1. What qualities must I have as the team leader?

2. How will I win my team's support?

3. What do I have to do to make my team function efficiently?

4. What do I have to do to satisfy my team's needs and concerns?

5. What do my team members expect of me as their leader?

6. What do I expect of my team?

CHAPTER 8
GETTING INVOLVED

This chapter utilizes the skills the students have learned to tackle a real problem they face in school or in their community. Over the course of the first five sessions, they develop a project designed to deal with a problem the class thinks important. The students identify the problem, choose a solution, create a plan, and present their project to a committee for evaluation. They then learn how to promote their project in the last three sessions. This chapter utilizes all the skills the students have learned in this course to make a difference in their world.

SESSIONS

DEVELOPING A PROJECT

Articulating a Problem
Planning
Determining Our Resources
The Proposal
Presenting the Project

PROMOTING THE PROJECT

Establishing Contacts
Communicating with the Press
Interviews

ARTICULATING A PROBLEM

The first steps in making a difference are identifying an issue, and evaluating and clearly articulating a problem. This session teaches students how to evaluate a problem and introduces them to project planning.

OBJECTIVES

Upon completing this lesson, the students will have accomplished the following:

1. Articulated a problem they wish to solve or project they wish to undertake
2. Justified their choice

MATERIALS NEEDED

Project Flowchart (copy for each student)
Planning a Project (copy for each student)

TEACHER TIPS

One of the main goals of this section is to show students that they can use the skills they have developed to solve actual problems, so make sure that the students' choices and all the steps they take in this chapter are grounded in reality. Remember to build on the enthusiasm of the group—it will keep the class moving forward, even if portions of the project are difficult. Do not discourage any suggestions; instead, point them in a practical direction. At the end of the project, students will present their projects to a committee for judging. Assemble the committee early and try to involve people from the larger community.

In this session, let all groups speak, even if two have chosen the same problem. The groups may have come to the same decision based on different arguments, and listening to the presentations will give the class a more complete understanding of the issue.

ACTIVITY

Part 1: Determining the Problem

1. Ask the students to list the important problems they face. Make sure these are problems they can do something about. Write these problems on the board. The students may refer to the list they made during the session Challenges (page 85) or they may list new problems.

2. Tell the students that they are to determine which problem they would like to try to solve as a class project. Ask the class to review the problems on the master list to see what would be involved in solving them. After the review, ask the class to vote for three problems they want as the class project.
3. Divide the class into three groups: society, our class, and independent experts. Ask them to choose the most significant of the three problems from the perspective of their group.
4. Following the presentations, have the class vote. Ask the students to justify their choice. Write the major arguments for choosing the problem on the board and ask the students to take notes as you discuss their choice.
5. Have the students choose a title for their project.
6. Appoint a committee to develop a concise definition of the problem and summarize the arguments for the project based on their notes. Ask the committee to put them in final form for distribution to the entire class under the title of the project. Remind the students to keep the summaries for future reference.

Part 2: Starting

1. Tell the students that in the next sessions they will be putting the skills they have learned into practice to solve the problem they have chosen. Acting in teams, they will analyze the problem and create a detailed proposal for solving it. The teams will then develop written proposals describing their plans, which they will present to a committee. The committee will determine which team has the best proposal.
2. Distribute Project Flowchart and review what will happen in the next few lessons.
3. Distribute Planning a Project and discuss the steps in developing a project.
4. Remind the students to keep the two handouts for future reference.

Project Flowchart

Select Problem

Develop a Solution

Plan the Project

Determine the Resources

Write a Proposal

Develop an Oral Presentation

Planning a Project

1. Articulate the Problem

Develop a clear, concise definition of the problem on which all can agree.

2. Define Your Objectives

- Be very specific about the objectives. Make sure that everyone agrees on the goals; conflicting goals can doom a project.
- Write a mission statement (a succinct statement of goals or purpose).

3. Analyze Scope and Constraints

- Be very clear about the project's scope. Different scopes have different implications for what must be done.
  - Time in which the project must be completed
  - Tasks
  - Overall implementation
- Constraints—be clear about the constraints you face. These will affect what you can accomplish. Some of the constraints to consider are
  - Participants' schedules
  - Conflicting obligations

4. Develop a Plan

- Be realistic about what you can accomplish in the time frame given.
- Outline each specific step you need to achieve your goal.
- Note any steps that are interdependent.
- Develop a realistic estimate of how long each step will take.
- Determine how you will monitor the progress of your project.
- Assign each task.

5. Determine Your Resources

- Review each step in your plan to determine what resources you will need to accomplish your goal.
- Determine how you will get these resources and who is responsible for acquiring them.
- If necessary, adjust the plan to fit the resources available.

6. Implement the Plan

- Monitor the progress of the plan and if necessary adjust it to fit the actual situation.

PLANNING

In this session, the students brainstorm ideas for solving the problem and develop a written plan, clearly articulating how they intend to reach their goal.

OBJECTIVES

Upon completing this lesson, the students will be able to do the following:

1. Understand the steps involved in planning a project
2. Create concrete plans for developing their project

MATERIALS NEEDED

Planning a Project (from the previous lesson)
Problem summary (developed in previous lesson)
Initial Planning activity sheet (copy for each student)

ACTIVITY

1. Divide the class into three or four groups. Tell the students that they will be working on the project as teams.
2. Ask the students to review Planning a Project from the previous lesson. Focus on the initial steps in planning: defining the objectives and developing the plan.
3. Ask the students to review the problem summary the committee developed in the last lesson. Distribute Initial Planning activity sheet and review.
4. Tell the teams that their first task will be to develop a common mission statement based on their teams' goals. Remind them of the definition of "mission statement" (a succinct statement of goals or purpose). Ask the team members to brainstorm a list of goals needed to solve the class problem. Remind them not to evaluate the ideas at this time. They are to just write down the goals the team members think important.
5. Ask the teams to identify the conflicts among the goals and settle them before proceeding. Do the team members have to make choices or compromise? If so, they must do so at this stage.
6. Based on their analysis, ask the teams to write their mission statements.
7. Once the teams have prepared their mission statements, ask the team members to discuss the scope of their project and any constraints they think they have to consider.
8. Ask the team members to determine what they can realistically accomplish and adjust their mission statement if necessary.
9. Tell the teams to list the specific tasks necessary to achieve their goal as well as the anticipated outcome for each. Ask them to assign the tasks to team members with dates for completion.

Activity Sheet

Initial Planning

INITIAL STEPS IN PLANNING

A. Defining Your Objectives

1. Brainstorm common goals.
2. Identify conflicts and make choices.
3. Decide which goals are achievable.
4. Based on your findings in steps 1–3, construct a mission statement. What do you want to accomplish? Write your mission statement on the following page.

B. Defining the Scope of the Project

1. Determine the scope of the project: the time by which your team must complete the project and the tasks it must accomplish.
2. List the constraints you face.
3. Determine what your team can realistically accomplish given the time frame and the constraints.
4. Outline the steps you need to achieve your goal and the outcomes you expect for each. Write them on the following page.
5. Determine a completion date for each and include it in the table.
6. Assign each task and write the name of the person responsible in the table.
7. Make sure each person has a clear understanding of what is required.

Our Project

MISSION STATEMENT

STEPS TO OUR GOAL

Step	Anticipated Outcome	Completion Date	Individual Assigned
1.			
2.			
3.			
4.			
5.			
6.			
7.			
8.			

DETERMINING OUR RESOURCES

In this lesson the teams determine the resources they need to develop their project. Team members assess the skills they could contribute and analyze where they might find the skills and other resources they are missing. In the process, they form a deeper understanding of what they have learned earlier—people must work together to make change happen.

OBJECTIVES

Upon completing this lesson, the students will have the following capabilities:

1. Be able to think creatively about where to find resources
2. Understand that they have a wide range of resources available
3. Be able to organize resources to accomplish a project

MATERIALS NEEDED

Completed Initial Planning activity sheets from previous lesson
Resources activity sheet (copy for each student)

TEACHER TIPS

One of the main goals of this lesson is for students to think creatively about the resources that surround them. Remind them to think beyond the school to their community and to the resources that may be available in libraries or on the Internet.

ACTIVITY

1. Assemble the teams and distribute Resources activity sheet. Have each review the plans that they drew up for the project in the previous lesson. Based on the plans, ask the teams to list the resources needed for each step. Remind the teams that the resources can be materials or people.
2. Have the teams enter the resources needed in the appropriate column of Resources activity sheet. Tell each team to determine where they might get the resources they need. Remind the students that they do not have to limit themselves to their group or even their class or school. Encourage them to think of the resources they can get from the larger community.
3. On the basis of their findings, ask the teams to evaluate whether they can reasonably assume that they can acquire the resources they need. If they cannot, tell them to determine whether they must adjust their plan.
4. Once the students have developed their final resource list, tell them to assign members of their team the task of acquiring the resources. Remind them to give the team members a time frame for completing the task.

Activity Sheet

Resources

Instructions:

1. Write the resources you will need for your project in the first column.
2. Indicate where you will get them in the second column. Remember to be specific.
3. Indicate who will get them in the third column.
4. Assign a date by which the team will have the resources in the fourth column.

Resources Needed	Where We Can Get Them	Who Will Get Them	Date by which We Will Have the Resource
1.			
2.			
3.			
4.			
5.			
6.			
7.			
8.			

THE PROPOSAL

This session teaches students how to write the formal proposal that will accompany their project presentation. They will learn how to summarize their case and to present the evidence they need to justify their plan. This exercise serves not only as an overview of their project but also as a final review of the assumptions and logic on which they based their plans.

OBJECTIVES

Upon completing this lesson, students will do the following:

1. Understand the steps involved in developing a formal proposal
2. Write a formal proposal

MATERIALS NEEDED

Components of a Proposal (copy for each student)

TEACHER TIPS

Regardless of how students approach the writing, they may find it easier to write the summary and conclusion after they have completed the other sections.

ACTIVITY

1. Assemble the teams. Tell the students that each team will be developing a written proposal describing its project.
2. Distribute Components of a Proposal and review carefully. Make sure that the students understand what is involved in each step of the process.
3. Ask each team to develop a draft of their proposal. Team members may work together or assign a different member to complete each section. If they work together, caution them to complete one section before they move on to the next.
4. Once the teams have their draft proposals, tell them to review and edit their documents.
5. Ask the teams to submit their drafts to you. Review them with each team and make suggestions for improvement.
6. Tell the teams to rework their documents until they are satisfied. Remind them that professional authors go through at least five drafts.
7. Ask the teams to submit their final proposals for review by the committee. You may want to review the proposals one more time before the teams formally submit them.

Components of a Proposal

1. PROJECT TITLE

Put this on a separate title page.

2. SUMMARY

Concise statement of your case (its goals and objectives). This page is the most important section of your proposal. It provides the reader with an overview of the key information in the proposal and attempts to convince the reader to support the project. Remember to include the problem and your solution.

3. STATEMENT OF NEED

Explains why this project is necessary. This section offers more information about the problem you introduced in the summary. It presents the arguments and evidence that support the need for the project. Remember to present the arguments in a logical order.

4. PROJECT TARGET

Explains who will benefit from the project.

5. PROJECT DESCRIPTION

The nuts and bolts of how the project will be implemented and evaluated. This section should include the following:
Objectives: the goal of the project, what the project will achieve
Methods: the specific activities that will take place to achieve the objective
Resources: what you need in terms of materials, skills, and financing to reach the goal
Evaluation: how you will evaluate the success of the project
Sustainability: how you will sustain the project once it has begun

6. CONCLUSION

Summary of the proposal's main points.

PRESENTING THE PROJECT

As a final step in the project, the teams present their plans to a committee, which will evaluate them and determine which proposal to adopt. This section of the process enables the students to extend the oral communication skills developed in earlier lessons.

OBJECTIVES

Upon completing this lesson, students will be able to do the following:

1. Understand the steps involved in developing a formal oral presentation
2. Make a formal oral presentation

MATERIALS NEEDED

Developing a Presentation resource sheet (copy for each student)
Speech Outline (copy for each student)
Tips for Presenting a Speech (copy for each student)

TEACHER TIPS

Try to include members of the wider community in the evaluation committee. Make sure that they have read each team's proposal before the oral presentations begin.

In the preparation phase of this assignment, remind students to practice and edit their presentation as often as time allows.

ACTIVITY

1. Assemble the teams. Tell the teams that they will be making 10-minute oral presentations before the committee to accompany their written proposals. The presentations will include a 5-minute speech and 5 minutes of question time for the panel.
2. Distribute Developing a Presentation resource sheet and Speech Outline and review carefully.
3. Ask the teams to develop outlines of their speeches. When they have finished, they are to submit the outlines to you for evaluation.
4. Once you have accepted the outlines, distribute Tips for Presenting a Speech and discuss.
5. Ask the teams to select one member as their spokesperson. Have the spokespersons work with their teams to develop their speeches.
6. Once the spokespersons are satisfied with their speeches, have them practice—ALOUD—with their groups. Ask the groups to critique the speech and edit if necessary. Remind the teams to repeat this process several times—until the spokespersons feel comfortable making the presentation.

7. Review each speech and make suggestions for improvement before the final formal presentation. Make sure the speeches fit into the 5-minute time frame
8. Schedule the presentations. Give each team 5 minutes to present its proposal. The panel then has 5 minutes to ask questions of the team's representative.
9. Based on the written proposals and oral presentations, have the panel recommend which proposal to pursue. The panel may suggest incorporating elements of other proposals in the one it accepts, or it may think all proposals of equal value.

Resource Sheet

Developing a Presentation

BEFORE DEVELOPING YOUR PRESENTATION

Consider the following:

- What is the purpose of my presentation? Articulating your goals helps you clarify your position and organize the arguments to support it.
- Who is the audience? If you know who your audience is, you can focus your presentation on the aspects of an issue that are important to your listeners.
- What arguments will best address the diverse viewpoints of the audience? Answering this question enables you to tailor your presentation so that your audience can identify with your argument and conclusions. Tolerance dictates that you consider not only your own opinion but also the opinions of others.
- What evidence do I need to support my arguments? Compile the data, statistics, etc. that will help you justify each of your arguments.

ORGANIZING A PRESENTATION

Presentations can be organized in many ways. Below is the most common one.

Introduction

Introduces members of the audience to the problem.

Makes them want to hear more about the problem by explaining how it impacts them or their community.

Sets the stage for the rest of your speech.

Thesis

States your solution to the problem.

Preview/Transition

Summarizes the main points you will present.

Body

Point 1 and support: Provides details of your plan. What specifically is your plan? Who will administer it? What will it cost?

Point 2 and support: Shows that the plan will work: it will achieve your goal. Provide concrete evidence—examples, statistics, testimonials.

Point 3 and support: Shows that the plan is desirable: it will benefit the audience or a segment of the community.

Conclusion

Wraps up your speech. Reminds your audience of all the reasons why they should accept your proposal.

GOALS FOR AN ORAL PRESENTATION

1. **Clarity and comprehension:** The audience needs to understand what you say.
2. **Credibility:** Good delivery makes the audience want to believe you.
3. **Memorability:** You want the audience to remember what you said.

Speech Outline

TITLE:

INTENTION:

Introduction

Thesis

Preview/Transition

BODY

Point 1:

Evidence:

Point 2:

Evidence:

Point 3:

Evidence:

CONCLUSION

Tips for Presenting a Speech

THE SPEECH

- Begin with a clever attention getter.
- Make sure your thesis is strong.
- Each argument in support of your thesis should be independent and supported by ample evidence.
- Ideas should be connected through logical transitions.
- Make sure you leave the audience with a memorable message.

PHYSICAL EXPRESSION

- Maintain eye contact with entire audience.
- Maintain strong posture, indicating you are purposeful and in command.
- Use gestures and movements to enhance your presentation but keep them natural and effective.

VOCAL EXPRESSION

- Use natural voice, not one that is patterned or monotone.
- Speak at a rate and volume that is similar to your normal speech.
- Use tone that is conversational but with purpose.
- Pronounce words clearly and correctly.

ESTABLISHING CONTACTS

In working on their projects, students learned that they could solve real problems in their school or neighborhood. But if they are to be responsible citizens, they must not merely propose solutions, they must also work to implement them. To do so, they must advocate their programs in the larger community. They must work with administrators, officials, and members of civil organizations to effect change. This lesson and the two that follow outline the steps the students will need to promote their programs effectively.

OBJECTIVES

Upon completing this lesson, the students will understand the steps necessary to contact the administrators and officials they will need to help them implement their projects.

MATERIALS NEEDED

Establishing Contacts resource sheet (copy for each student)
Meeting with Community Contacts resource sheet (copy for each student)
Accepted proposal (copy for each student)

TEACHER TIPS

Make sure that the students research real groups and individuals. Although they will not be actually contacting these individuals, the students should learn how to navigate a bureaucracy. The Internet can be extremely helpful in researching this lesson.

ACTIVITY

1. Tell the students that they cannot stop with the adoption of a proposal. In order to affect change, they must implement their plan. To do so, they must involve the larger community. They must contact the administrators and officials whose help they will need to realize their goal and the public whose backing ensures that officials will act.
2. Organize the class into teams. Distribute Establishing Contacts resource sheet and review.
3. Ask the students to research the contacts they will need to implement the approved project and prepare their materials for the interview.
4. Once the students have completed their research, distribute Meeting with Community Contacts resource sheet and discuss. Assign students to be "officials." (You will need an official for

each team.) Form contact pairs by asking each team to select a representative who will present its plan and pairing that person with an official. Make sure that the official is not from the same team as the representative. The remaining students are observers; divide them evenly among the contact pairs. The observers are to take notes on the interview, indicating strengths and weaknesses.

5. Ask the pairs to conduct their interviews. Have officials, representatives, and observers report their impressions to the class.

DISCUSSION QUESTIONS

1. Why is it important to have a clear understanding of the goal of the interview throughout the contact process?
2. What was the most difficult part of researching the appropriate contacts?
3. What was the most challenging part of the interview?

Resource Sheet

Establishing Contacts

Step 1. Determine Your Goals

- What is the goal of your communication?
    - Advertising a project
    - Gaining support for the proposal
    - Involving local authorities in your activities
    - Using local authorities for fundraising
- What is the scope of your activities?
    - Local
    - Regional
    - National
    - International
- What is the duration of your communication?
    - Short time
    - Long time
    - Periodic—related to projects run by our assembly

Step 2. Identify Your Contacts

Based on the answers above

- What specific groups should you contact?
- What branch or department within each group can help you? Who should you contact (be specific)?
- What specifically do you want these individuals to do?

Step 3. Review Your Proposal

Make sure that your proposal is complete and that it contains important contact information:

Name

Address

Telephone number

Fax number

E-mail address

Step 4. Contact the Official

Contact the official by e-mail or telephone to make an appointment. The official's administrative assistant will explain the best way to proceed. Have your proposal ready to fax or mail if requested or for reference during your conversation.

Meeting with Community Contacts

Basic Rules

1. Always be punctual. Give yourself plenty of time to get to the meeting.
2. Dress properly. You most likely will be in a formal business situation.
3. Be respectful and polite. Introduce yourself to the official and shake her hand.
4. Have a pre-prepared presentation that you can leave with your contact.
5. Keep your goal in mind throughout the interview.
6. Remember to present your main points in a concise fashion. The official's time is valuable.
7. Be an equal partner in the conversation: do not dominate and do not allow yourself to be dominated.
8. Before you leave, ask how you can maintain contact.
9. Remember to thank the person you speak with at the close of the meeting.

COMMUNICATING WITH THE PRESS

Publicizing the students' project is vital to bringing it into the "real world" where it can effect change. This teaches the students how to publicize their project effectively in newspapers and on radio and television.

OBJECTIVES

Upon completing this lesson, the students will understand the following:

1. The importance of using the press to publicize their program
2. How to work effectively with the press

MATERIALS NEEDED

Press Release Questions resource sheet (copy for each student)
Template for a Press Release resource sheet (copy for each student)
Accepted proposal (copy for each student)

TEACHER TIPS

You might want to invite a reporter or editor to discuss the most effective ways to establish and maintain contact with the press.

ACTIVITY

Divide the students into teams and have them review the accepted proposal.

1. Explain to the students that one of the most effective ways to let the press know about their project is to develop a press release. This gives reporters a summary of the project and ensures that they have accurate information about it when writing their stories.
2. Distribute Press Release Questions resource sheet and discuss.
3. Ask each group to answer the questions about the project.
4. Distribute Template for a Press Release resource sheet and discuss. Ask each team to use the template to write a press release about the project.
5. Have the teams distribute their releases to the class and discuss.

DISCUSSION QUESTIONS

1. Why is it important to use catchy words for your title?
2. Why is it important to be concise?
3. A famous author once said, "I can write three bad pages or one good page a day." Relate this quote to writing a press release.

Resource Sheet

Press Release Questions

Your press release should answer the following questions:

1. What is the most important fact your press release aims to get across?
2. Does your press release contain the following?
   - Who
   - What
   - Where
   - When
   - How
   - Why
3. What are the challenges and goals of your project?
4. Are there any specific challenges for which the project needs help to succeed?
5. Are there any other newsworthy aspects of your project that you can include?

Resource Sheet

Template for a Press Release

Opening Wording: Insert the words NEWS RELEASE, in capital letters, about two inches below your letterhead.

Release Time: Place this under NEWS RELEASE. There are two options:
FOR IMMEDIATE RELEASE (if the release can be published immediately)
HOLD FOR RELEASE UNTIL ____ (the time you wish the outlet to publish it)

Target: Indicate who the intended recipient is, e.g., ATTENTION EDUCATION EDITOR.

Headline: Keep your headline short and catchy. Use capital letters.

Date and Location: Enter the date you will be distributing the release and the location from where you will be releasing the announcement.

Introductory Paragraph: Create an interest-catching introduction that answers some or all of the questions: who, what, where, when, how, and why.

Second and Subsequent Paragraphs: Briefly describe the project and its significance.

For Further Information: Tell the media whom they can contact to follow up. Provide name, address, telephone number, e-mail address.

Sample Press Release Format

PROJECT RENEW
MIDDLETOWN HIGH SCHOOL

NEWS RELEASE
FOR IMMEDIATE RELEASE
ATTENTION EDUCATION EDITOR

PROJECT RENEW SOLVES WASTEPAPER PROBLEM

December 12, 2005, Oakton, MN

(first paragraph)

(Body of Release)

Contact:
John Roberts
Middletown High School
1313 1st St.
Oakton, MN 44444
(555) 555-5555
xvzy@mhsmn.edu

INTERVIEWS

Students will also want to publicize their projects through media interviews. They are not likely to get network coverage, but they may be able to organize a local radio interview. This session presents the basic information they need to conduct a successful interview.

OBJECTIVES

Upon completing this lesson, students will understand how to prepare for a media interview.

MATERIALS NEEDED

Preparing for a Media Interview resource sheet (copy for each student)
Accepted proposal (copy for each student)

ACTIVITY

Part 1: Preparing for the Interview

1. Explain that one effective way students can promote their projects is through media interviews. These interviews can be exciting but also challenging, and so the people being interviewed must be well prepared.
2. Have the class create profiles of three or four radio or TV programs: what type of media outlets are they; who are their audiences (what are the audience demographics, are they trying to appeal to a specific section of the political spectrum, etc.). Name each program and write these descriptions on the board.
3. Ask for volunteers to be interviewers or assign the role. You will need an interviewer for each team. Make sure that you have no more than one person from each team as interviewer.
4. Assign each interviewer a media profile (you can have duplicates) and a team (not their own), and remind them to review the accepted proposal.
5. Assemble the teams, and distribute Preparing for a Media Interview resource sheet and discuss.
6. While the interviewers review the proposal and prepare questions for a 10-minute interview, ask the teams to prepare the information required in Step 1 of the resource sheet.
7. Ask each team to choose a representative to be interviewed about the project.

Part 2: Interviews

1. Once the teams and interviewers have prepared the information, hold the interviews. Ask each interviewer to pair with the person she is to interview on her program. The remaining students are the audience and should be distributed evenly among the various programs. Try to make sure that the observers do not come from the same team as the person being interviewed.
2. Tell the observers to take notes on the interview, indicating what they think are the most interesting points. What made them excited about the project?
3. Following the interviews, have the participants in each program, including audience members, discuss the experience. Then, have the programs share their thoughts with the class.

DISCUSSION QUESTIONS

1. What was the most difficult part of the interview?
2. What do you need to make an interview successful?

Preparing for a Media Interview

Step 1: Before the Interview

Review your proposal.

Prepare your project's message:

- Identify the goal of your program.
- Identify three-to-four key points about your program.
- Identify the most controversial or interesting issues about your project.

Research the media outlet and the interviewer:

- Who is the general audience of the media outlet?
- What is the interviewer's background?
- What kind of questions is the interviewer likely to ask you?

Step 2: During the Interview

Presentation:

- Be clear.
- Be concise.
- Be honest.
- Correct mistakes if you make any.
- Admit if you do not know something.
- Break up complex questions into simpler ones.

Body language:

- Be relaxed but lively.
- Maintain eye contact with the interviewer.
- Avoid quick, unnecessary movements, particularly if this is a TV interview.
- Smile pleasantly.

Step 3: After the Interview

Thank the interviewer.